HISTORY OF MEN'S ETIQUETTE

A SHORT GUIDE TO THE SPORTING LIFE

This book is dedicated to the memory of Dolph and Mary Marshall and Margaret Downing.

For all the time you gave me.

From quiet homes and first beginning,
Out to the undiscovered ends,
There's nothing worth the wear of winning,
But laughter and the love of friends.

Hilaire Belloc

HISTORY OF
MEN'S ETIQUETTE

A Short Guide to the Sporting Life

by

NICHOLAS STOREY

First published in Great Britain in 2011 by
Remember When
an imprint of
Pen & Sword Books Ltd
47 Church Street
Barnsley
South Yorkshire
S70 2AS

ISBN 978 1 84468 114 3

Typeset in 11/13pt Baskerville by
Mac Style, Beverley, East Yorkshire

Printed and bound in the UK
by the MPG Books Group

Pen & Sword Books Ltd incorporates the Imprints of Pen & Sword Aviation,
Pen & Sword Family History, Pen & Sword Maritime, Pen & Sword Military,
Pen & Sword Discovery, Wharncliffe Local History, Wharncliffe True Crime,
Wharncliffe Transport, Pen & Sword Select, Pen & Sword Military Classics,
Leo Cooper, The Praetorian Press, Remember When, Seaforth Publishing and
Frontline Publishing.

For a complete list of Pen & Sword titles please contact
PEN & SWORD BOOKS LIMITED
47 Church Street, Barnsley, South Yorkshire, S70 2AS, England
E-mail: enquiries@pen-and-sword.co.uk
Website: www.pen-and-sword.co.uk

Contents

Acknowledgements and Permissions

I am immensely grateful, once again, for the generous help and advice on technical aspects of the draft chapters of this book from experts in the fields that I have covered. In chapter order, they are as follows. For reading and advising on sporting guns (excepting 'binoculars' and 'pest control') in chapter 1, I thank Roy Lyu, Gunroom Manager of Boss & Co, as well as for the illustrations that appear in Plates 3 to 6 inclusive (Plates 4 and 6 also appear on the cover). I also thank a private collector (who wishes to remain anonymous), for the use of the image in Plate 2 of the duelling pistols made by Robert Wogdon (which are in a private collection), and for reading over the section on duelling and duelling pistols in chapter 1.

For reading and advising on game fishing in chapter 2, I thank Edward Barder, as well as for the images in Plates 8 and 9 (Plate 9 also appears on the cover). For reading and advising on falconry in chapter 3 I thank both Jevgeni Shergalin, Archivist of The Falconry Trust (as well as for Plate 10), and Nick Kester. For reading and advising on hats (especially those for hunting), I thank Janet Taylor of Patey Hats, who has been, as ever, a rich source of valuable learning, generously shared; as well as for the images in Plates 12, 13 and 14. Likewise, I thank Douglas Simpson, of Ascot Hats Ltd, for sharing a store of accumulated information and records, concerning the first patenting of silk plush for hats in England and the origination of the first silk plush top hats there.

For reading and advising on roses in chapter 7 and for the image in Plate 22 I thank Peter Beales of Peter Beales Roses and for reading and advising on bees and bee-keeping, in the same chapter, I thank apiarist Mrs Karen Mann, of Crane Brook, St Margarets, Twickenham. For looking over the draft book as a whole I also thank: Dr Ron Collins, Laurence Mann (also for Plate 23); Dr Julian Critchlow; Chikashi Miyamoto, and Dr Marcelo d'Araujo of Laranjeiras. I thank as well, again, the whole team at Remember When; including my commissioning editor, Lisa Hooson, and my copy editor, Sue Blackhall.

Apart from those mentioned above, for kind permission to use other illustrations, in plate order, I thank the following:

Plate 7 – J Roberts & Son

For help with Plates 15, 16 and 19 and for the images in Plates 18 and 24, I thank my father.

Plate 17 – Erin Shipley, Westminster City Archives
Plate 20 – My cousins Brian and Susan Bazeley.

Plate 25 – Annamaria Duvia, of Villa D'Este, Lake Como.
Plate 26 – Joanna Kersley, of The Venice-Simplon-Orient Express.
Plate 27 – Martin Daly of The School Garage.
Plate 28 – Louis Lejeune Ltd.
Plate 29 – Mr TAD Crook, of Bristol Cars Ltd.
Plate 30 – Eva Reinecke of Badrutt's Palace Hotel, St. Moritz. This image also
          appears on the cover.

Additionally:
Plate 1 is from an original cartoon, by Thomas Rowlandson (1756–1827). It also
    appears on the cover.
Plate 10 is from an original illustration by Dr Afred E. Brehm (1829–1884),
    published in *Cassell's Book of Birds*, by Thomas Rymer Jones (1874).
Plate 11 is from the original painting of Lord Ribblesdale, by John Singer Sargent
    (1856–1925). It also appears on the cover.
Plate 15 is from an old engraving of Robert Coates, of unknown provenance.
Plate 16 is from an original cartoon, by George du Maurier (1834–1896),
    published in *Punch*, on 9 November 1895.
Plate 19 is from an original painting, by John Wootton (1682–1764).
Plate 21 is from an original '*Spy*' cartoon, by Sir Leslie Ward (1851–1922),
    published in *Vanity Fair*, on 29 June 1889.
Plate 31 is from an original cartoon poster by Elizabeth Pyke.

There are some glossaries of terms, which I have included in the text and not, in the more usual way, placed at the end of the book, because they contain terms which are relevant only to the passages of the book in which they appear and are not terms that appear throughout.

Following my general recent practice, there is no list of suppliers' contact details and, again, this is because these lists soon become dated. Most of the businesses (and other organizations) mentioned have their own websites (easily found through searching the business or organization names) and those few that do not may be found in the telephone directories. Sometimes, where businesses have websites, I have made use of some of the information to be found there.

Where clothing is discussed or might seem relevant, further detail is available in *History of Men's Fashion*, to which I occasionally make cross reference.

No one who has helped me with advice or illustrations should be taken, necessarily, to endorse any of the opinions that I express (including political opinions) and, although I have done my best to ensure that the draft has passed before renowned experts on the technical aspects of some of the things that I cover, for any remaining errors I alone am responsible.

Nicholas Storey,
Estado do Rio de Janeiro,
Brasil

Introduction

You never enjoy the world aright till the sea itself floweth in your veins, till you are clothed with the heavens and crowned with the stars.

The Rev. Thomas Traherne MA (born circa 1636, died 1674)

Whard Dr Samuel Johnson made his remark that…

'…there is in London all that life can afford…'

there were still, within easy walking distance of the Fleet Street off which he lived (variously in Gough Square, Inner Temple Lane, and Bolt Court), farms, open fields and, on them, country sporting activities. This is no longer true and London is, apart from modest areas of preserved and prettified parkland and some golf and sports' clubs, a vast conurbation; separated from the countryside and the pursuits that may be had there. This means that, to enjoy a fully rounded life, it is necessary to split one's time between town and country, according to the seasons and having regard to the events and activities in both places, as well as leavening each year's experience with travel as far and wide as possible.

This book is intended to be a further guide to the Good Life, in the sense of encouraging maximization of learning and enjoyment, without sacrificing virtue. It covers something about the basics of the main country sports and sporting equipment, including: shooting and shotguns and rifles, and fishing and fishing rods and equipment; hunting and hunting gear; tennis, croquet, badminton, squash and golf kit and some members' clubs (although I do not cover team sports and games, such as rowing, cricket, polo, soccer and rugby); town and country living, with some reference to real property and housing and some more thoughts on dress; town and country sporting and social events; road, rail and sea travel, as well as exciting or unusual Christmas holiday destinations. It ends with a reminiscence of an unforgettable night in London.

The intention is to produce a guide on the main subjects that complements my other books *History of Men's Fashion – What the Well Dressed Man is Wearing*

('*History of Men's Fashion*') and *History of Men's Accessories – A Short Guide For Men About Town* ('*Men About Town*'); both also published by Pen & Sword Books under the 'Remember When' imprint. As with these earlier books I hope that some glint of humour shows through and that (apart from safety considerations), no one takes any of my suggestions *too* earnestly. That some people do is reflected in the fact that I sent the draft on mounted hunts to someone involved at a high level in organizing mounted hunting and he described it as 'Draconian', which suggests that he has a seriously limited sense of humour. Fortunately, he did not say that anything was inaccurate in it as such. Certainly, my purpose is far from wishing to discourage participation in the sports and pursuits that I mention.

Again, I have to stress that this book is not exhaustive in relation to the topics covered and that it sets out my own ideas and thoughts and, if anyone might disdain the lightness of the coverage, my hope is that few will be able to find serious fault with the substance.

I mention various other organizations as I go along, in connection with specific activities, but always bear in mind also that there are The Countryside Alliance and The British Association For Shooting and Conservation, which do their level best to promote the preservation of the flora and fauna of the rural environment; the welfare of the people who dwell in it, and the countryside as a way of life, which tends to be misunderstood by the unfortunate people that I describe later as 'Urbanites'. These are organizations which deserve the full support of all those who are interested in the countryside.

Finally, I should add a word of explanation for the sentence that heads this Introduction. It is a golden sentence, penned by Thomas Traherne, who was a poor, Welsh curate of the seventeenth century, and might seem at odds with a book aimed at the sports and pursuits of the man of the world. However, let me assure you, out of my own experience that, if you have no essential, deep and grateful recognition of all the natural beauty in this world; in the sky and stars beyond, and appreciation of our little places in the great, unknown purpose of it all, then you will find contentment nowhere.

CHAPTER 1

Country Sports –
Guns and Shooting

There is a passion for hunting something deeply implanted in the human breast.

Charles Dickens

Some history of hunting and of duelling with guns

From one small spark springs up a mighty flare.

Paradiso, Canto 1 (Dante, translated by Dorothy L Sayers)

Incendiary devices of various kinds have been combined with offensive projectiles for many centuries but a crude gunpowder was the invention of the Chinese in around AD 850 (some alchemists had been seeking an elixir). The first European description of it seems to have been by an English monk, called Roger Bacon, in 1249. This ingenious fellow even seems to have been ahead of Leonardo da Vinci in his prediction of future inventions, such as flying machines. Gunpowder was first put to use in cannon by about 1320 but it wasn't until the fifteenth century that (manually ignited) shoulder guns were devised. In 1520 the flintlock mechanism (flint sparking on steel, sometimes causing misfires called a mere '*a flash in the pan*'), was invented in Spain and, by the sixteenth century, the English Parliament thought it necessary to regulate the use of cross bows and guns.

The muzzle-loading guns of this period were single-barrelled but in the seventeenth century double-barrelled guns, in the over-and-under configuration, were devised.

Until 1750 it was rare for game to be taken by shooting in the air since the guns simply were not fast and accurate enough. Once they became so, by the late eighteenth century, some estates had begun to breed pheasants for release as aerial targets. By the end of the eighteenth century, English gunmakers of

'Best London Guns' (or *'London Best Guns'*), were coming to the leading position that they have maintained ever since.

One of the greatest gun-makers of these times was Joseph Manton (born circa 1766, died in 1835). He opened his shop in 1793 and began turning out light, graceful, understated, magnificently engraved pieces, with octagonal barrels and stamped with a tiger badge. Others copied the innovations in design. Forced into bankruptcy in 1826 by the government's refusal to pay up on munitions' contracts, his acolytes struck out on their own and their businesses are still with us: Thomas Boss; James Purdey; Joseph Lang (from 1821 Atkin, Grant & Lang); William Greener (WW Greener), and Charles Lancaster. They maintain the fine traditions of this broken-down genius, whose own work still attracts a large premium at auction. Joseph had been apprenticed to his elder brother, John, whose own business continued to survive and indeed enjoyed the patronage of the Prince Consort. The John Manton Best guns are marked 'John Manton & Son'. There are some other guns marked 'J Manton & Co' but these are cheap imports.

Durs Egg and John Twigg were a couple of the Mantons' rivals (especially noted for fine duelling pistols), as well as John Rigby (founded in Dublin, Ireland in 1735), and Henry Nock (founded in 1772), who was given a royal warrant by George III in 1804. This firm, taken over, on his death, by Nock's son-in-law, James Wilkinson, branched out into bayonets and blades and became even more famous as sword cutler Wilkinson Sword. Wogdon & Barton was another firm and Robert Wogdon's duelling pistols had claimed so many men's lives that he was the subject of a verse in 1783, which began:

> 'Hail, Wogdon! Patron of that leaden death,
> Which awaits alike the bully and the brave.'

Other great makers of the time included HW Mortimer, and Joseph Griffin.

A side-note on duelling and duelling pistols

Any wound sufficient to agitate the nerves and make the hand shake must end the business for that day.

> Commandment Twenty One of the Twenty Six
> Commandments of the (Irish) Code Duello of 1777

Duelling with weapons had long been regarded, in the British Isles (and, later, in the British Colonies), as well as in parts of Europe, as the only way for gentlemen to settle points of honour; that is to say points of difference between men which reflected adversely on the character of a gentleman to sit back and take it; largely centred on calumnious utterances. This flowed from the earliest method of settling disputes (including certain property disputes, which would nowadays be dealt with in a modern judicial forum): trial by battle; all influenced, to some extent by the tournaments of medieval knights and the throwing down of the gauntlet to initiate a challenge. At least until Lords Queensbury and Lonsdale became involved in the regulation of the competitive sport of boxing, simple fisticuffs were regarded as the recourse of the rabble. The Queensbury Rules of boxing date from 1867 and the Lonsdale prize boxing belts were launched in 1909.

In 1777, the Irish devised the *Twenty Six Commandments of the Code Duelo*, which strictly regulated the conduct of the duel; to ensure, most importantly: that no duel took place in hot blood; that there were intermediaries ('Seconds') appointed to make the arrangements, including the investigation whether an honourable retraction and apology might not suffice and to ensure fair play in the event of action. However, occasionally, the Seconds disagreed and then they would fight their own duel simultaneously and at right-angles with the Principals!

As a matter of interest, the first recorded pistol duel was fought on Tothill Fields in 1711 and, as swordsmanship declined, gradually, pistols became the weapon of choice and, although even taking proper aim was frowned upon as not being *insouciant* enough, some makers introduced unsportsmanlike rifled barrels. Manton produced heavier pistols, weighted at the muzzle, to counteract the recoil; hair triggers and better balanced weapons were not regarded as unsportsmanlike. Duelling continued to be tolerated as the recognized manner of settling points of honour between gentlemen: for example, on 6 April 1803, at 7pm, on Primrose Hill, Lieutenant-Colonel Sir William Montgomery of Magbiehill, Bart., met Captain Macnamara RN to settle a dispute between them arising out of the fact that their dogs had quarrelled and fought in Hyde Park. Both were injured by the exchange of fire but Montgomery died on the spot and Macnamara was tried for murder but acquitted because the jury decided that the duel had been fairly conducted. Others were not so lucky and a conviction for murder was a risk of killing a duelling opponent. Lesser charges for wounding were also a possibility as the 7th Earl of Cardigan discovered (he was later commander of the Light Brigade in its famous charge at the Battle of Balaklava in 1854). He had been the subject of a critical article in the *Morning Chronicle*, written (about petty disputes in the mess and Cardigan's harsh handling of them), by one of his fellow officers, Captain Harvey Tuckett. Cardigan had already been subject to ridicule for disciplining an officer who ordered a black bottle (actually of wine) to the mess table, against Cardigan's order that no black bottles (normally containing porter) might appear in the mess. Cardigan challenged Tuckett and they met on Wimbledon Common on 12 September 1840. At the second shot, Cardigan wounded Tuckett (with a shot from an unsportsmanlike rifled barrel), and was then arrested for unlawful wounding. He elected to be tried, as was then his right, "By God and my peers" in the House of Lords. Despite his use of the unsporting rifled barrel, he was acquitted on the exiguous technicality that there was some doubt over the precise statement of the victim's name in the Indictment. Why on earth such a trivial error could not have been amended is unclear and it all shows that, so far as a trial for duelling is concerned, Cardigan probably could not have asked for a more sympathetic tribunal.

Even Prime Ministers in office, had fought duels. In 1798 William Pitt The Younger, annoyed by an Irish MP over Naval quotas, challenged his loyalty to the Crown and, at 3 pm on 27 May 1798, they met at twelve paces on Putney Heath and both fired and both missed. The 1st Duke of Wellington, as Tory Prime Minister, forced the issue of Roman Catholic 'Emancipation', pushing through legislation to enable Roman Catholics to hold certain public offices (from which they had previously been barred); in an effort to quell Irish unrest. The Earl of Winchilsea criticized him heavily and they faced each other on Battersea Fields on 21 March 1829. Winchilsea fired into the air and Wellington shot wide, accepting a written apology, instead of blood. Meanwhile a more widely criticized affair had been the duel between Lord Castlereagh (then Secretary of State for War) and George Canning (then Foreign Secretary). Castlereagh accused Canning of extreme political intrigue and they both resigned office and met on Putney Heath on 21 September 1809. Canning missed and Castlereagh wounded Canning in the leg. Canning went on to become, briefly, Prime Minister in 1827, while the extremely unpopular Castlereagh killed himself with a penknife in 1822. According to a contemporary popular verse, from *The Mask of Anarchy* by PB Shelley (referring to Castlereagh's responsibility for a murderous cavalry charge at St Peter's Fields, Manchester, in August 1819 ('The Peterloo Massacre') to disperse a crowd of radicals):

> 'I met Murder on the way,
> He had a mask like Castlereagh.'

Even the young Abraham Lincoln was drawn into a duel with an Illinois politician called James Shields, who accused Lincoln of writing, or being behind, calumnious, anonymous letters in the press about Shields. They met near the Mississippi River, in Missouri, on 22 September 1842 and their Seconds attempted to compromise the matter but Shields initially resisted until he realized that Lincoln's reach with his sabre was much greater than his own. The matter was then settled and the two even appear to have become friends.

A duelling cartoon, by Thomas Rowlandson, is shown in Plate 1.

Duelling between civilians (as well as the ancient remedy of trial by battle) was specifically banned in Britain in 1819 and duelling between commissioned officers was banned in 1844. Despite this, the last reported duel in England took place, in 1852, at Priest Hill, Surrey, between two Frenchmen, called Cournet and Bartlemey. Cournet took his shot and missed; Bartlemey's pistol misfired twice and Cournet lent him his own weapon (maybe expecting the gallantry to be repaid by *delopement* – discharge of the gun in the air) but, instead, Bartlemey mortally wounded Cournet with it! In the event, they both died as a result of the duel, as Bartlemey was soon hanged for murder.

Cased pairs of fine duelling pieces are eminently collectable and they are sometimes offered at auction by houses such as Bonham's, Holt's and Christie's. A fine pair by Robert Wogdon, in a private collection, is shown in Plate 2.

Further development of firearms

Percussion locks were invented by Alexander Forsyth in 1807, and had a serious impact on the old muzzle-loading method. In 1840 M Lefaucheux of Paris devised a pinfire gun, brought to England by J Lang in 1851. In around 1860 the central fire system arrived. Breech-loaders were taken to a high state of the art in the 1860s but they still had external hammers, which had disadvantages in terms of speed and safety in the field.

The first 'hammerless' guns were perfected from the designs of William Anson and John Deeley (respectively gunmaker and managing director at the firm of Westley Richards), and patented in 1875. The simplified action of the boxlock was the result. It isn't really hammerless at all; it's just that the tumblers (or hammers) are hidden inside the central part of the action. In short, in modern versions, there is a cocking lever, a mainspring, the tumblers (hammers) and the sears that are sprung by the triggers to release the tumblers to detonate the cartridges. An advantage of this is that the hammers are not exposed to accidents and damage. The action was later (ingeniously) made self-cocking, from the opening of the gun at the breach for loading. The gun is opened with a lever on the top of the action, behind the fences. There may be either a front trigger for the right barrel and a back trigger for the left barrel or a single selective trigger (for both barrels), which is selected by a switch. In Plates 3 and 4 is a Boss over and under shotgun displaying a single selective trigger. Sprung, self-opening guns were an innovation dating from 1880 and, from 1882, a trigger-block safety catch was generally fitted as standard. From 1890, there have also been automatic cartridge ejectors.

Sidelocks are similar to boxlocks in design but, instead of the action being in the centre of the action chamber, it is found beneath each of the side-plates. These are more expensive to produce than boxlocks and any clear advantage in the sporting field is doubtful.

The best guns have chopper lump (or demi-bloc) barrels, which is a method of joining the barrels with integrated steel in the forging. Other methods are the dovetail lump method and the platform lump method (the latter being the most common method in general shotgun production).

Glossary of gun and shooting terms

Acier Cockerill – A maker of fluid steel for gun barrels (rather than Damascus steel).

Anti-recoil pad – Pad fitted to the shoulder end of the stock to absorb the kick.

Action – A gun's action comprises the receiver (frame) and the breech locking and firing mechanisms and is the heart of the gun.

Best London guns (or London Best guns) – Top of the range guns, which traditionally have sidelock actions, intercepting sears (safety features), chopper lump barrels, locks concealed in the floorplate and are 'stocked to the fences' (an expression sometimes also used to denote other things that have been very well made).

Bluing – The barrels of guns are blued by a chemical process which causes the surface steel to produce magnetite, the black oxide of iron, for cosmetic purposes and to help prevent the formation of destructive rust, the red oxide of iron. Barrels still need to be oiled to provide additional protection.

Bore – In the UK this means the weight, in fractions of a pound of a solid sphere of lead which is the diameter of the inside of the barrel. Therefore a 12 bore is bigger than a 20 bore as one twelfth of a pound is more than one twentieth. One anomaly is the .410 gauge which is simply equivalent to an internal diameter of .410 of an inch. The lighter 20 bore and the .410 were, generally speaking, guns for youngsters and the ladies but now that over and under shotguns are making headway in the sporting field (and as they are generally heavier than side-by-sides), the smaller bores are becoming popular across the board.

Boxlock – See further development of firearms above.

Breech – The end of the barrels nearer the stock.

Calibre – Rifles and handguns are measured in calibre, which is just the diameter (sometimes measured in fractions of an inch and sometimes in millimetres), of the gun barrel and the projectile that it fires (a bullet from a cartridge). One famous, dangerous game cartridge is the Rigby .416, devised by the firm of John Rigby & Co in 1911, for use in rifles that were specially made to enable fast reloading to dispatch enraged, wounded animals. The .375 Holland & Holland calibre is now a standard calibre and (although a large calibre for deer), can be used with 235–270 grain bullets for deer or with 300 grain bullets for big game. (A grain is a unit of weight used for bullets and gold and there are just nearly fifteen and a half grains in one gram.)

Cartridges – Comprise casing, primer, powder, wad and shot and another wad. Modern smokeless powders, including nitro-glycerine, have taken the place of the original 'black powder'. The shot is normally lead but there are moves in various countries to prevent the use of lead shot over water, for environmental reasons (because lead shot and lost lead fishing weights poison flora and fauna), and steel, tungsten and bismuth composite shot are being manufactured for this reason. Care needs to be exercised (and advice taken), in using new, composite shot in old guns as they were built and proofed for lead. New gun barrels can be bespoken that are compatible with steel-shot. The shot pellets in the shells will vary in size, according to the range of the shooting and the type of game involved. A good all round size for pheasant and general walked-up shooting is 4–6 shot size but you would move to size 2–4 for high-flying waterfowl; not least because the feathering on these birds is denser and more oiled than that on pheasants. As with 'bore' the smaller the number of the shot size, the larger the pellets. To determine the exact size of the pellets in the numbered shot, first deduct the shot size from seventeen; for example seventeen, less shot size two, equals fifteen; then divide this by one hundred; accordingly shot size two contains pellets that are each fifteen hundredths of an inch in diameter.

Case-hardened steel – Steel that has been treated to increase its hardness. The test for it is to run a file over it; if the file 'bites', the steel has not been case-hardened; if the file glides over the steel, then it has been. Not all steel that has been blued has, necessarily, been case-hardened too.

Cast-off – The built-in bias of a bespoke gun stock to account for right-handed shooting. Bias for a left-handed gun is 'cast-on'.

Comb of stock – The part of the stock next to the cheek.

Chamber – Action at the breech.

Chiselling – A method of decorating the fences of Best Guns, by chasing with a round wooden mallet and chisel, and gouges so that the carved decoration (often oak, ivy or fern leaves) is raised up in bas-relief. This is in comparison with the usual *intaglio* engraving of the sideplates.

Choke – The degree of constriction at the muzzle, which may be built in or removable (and, therefore, changeable). There are also offset chokes to

16

correct defective sight. The second barrel on side-by-sides and the upper barrel on over-and-unders is often choked to concentrate the shot from the cartridge and so give a longer range of shot; for use when, say, wildfowling. Clay guns often have various removable chokes for different ranges in competition shooting.

Combination gun – An over-and-under combination of rifle and shotgun barrels, for hunting where mixed game can be expected. There are even versions with three barrels (called a *drilling*) or four barrels (called a *vierling*).

Damascus steel barrels – Barrels made of laminations of pattern-welded, folded steel, producing (coincidentally), a moiré effect on the surface.

Damascus (or Damask) work – Etching over layers of different (Damascus) steels to produce patterns (damascened steel).

Droplock – Lock, detachable without tools, for cleaning; a speciality of Westley Richards.

Ejector – An automatic ejector.

Fences – Top back part of the external metal work behind the breech.

Full choke – Maximum constriction at the muzzle.

Gauge – Interior dimension of the bore.

Grain through hand – A straight grain of wood through the grip, for strength; as the wrist is the thinnest part of the stock.

Grip – The piece of the stock for the trigger hand and often incorporates a chequered pattern, scored into the wood at the rate of twenty two lines per square inch (it may be more or it may be less).

Gun slip – The light covers for carrying guns to and from the shooting ground.

Half pistol grip (Prince of Wales grip) – Chequered grip in a pistol shape in the stock.

Heel – Top of the back of the stock.

Hinge – Separates the barrels from the standing breech block.

Improved cylinder – The least constricted choke.

Leading the target – Shooting ahead of the target; when shooting uphill, shoot above it and, when shooting downhill, shoot below it.

Modified choke – Moderate barrel constriction.

Muzzle – Business end of the barrels.

Over-and-under configuration – Term for double barrels so arranged, as shown in the over and under shotgun, by Boss & Co, in Plates 3 and 4.

Proofed guns – Since the establishment of the trade guild of the Worshipful Company of Gunmakers, guns have been 'proofed', by Houses of Proof, to test their safety. This is done by submitting the guns to a stress greater than the normal stress to which they are subjected, according to current statutory regulation and control, under the Gun Barrel Proof Acts, 1868, 1950 and

1978 and Rules of Proof, made under them. The two Houses of Proof are the Company of Gunmakers in London and the Guardians of the Birmingham Proof House. Guns that are successfully proofed are stamped accordingly. Guns may also be re-proofed over time. Strict penalties are applied for infringing the rules, since unsafe guns can blow up in the user's face.

Receiver – The frame of the action.

Rib – Usually the concave distance along middle length between the barrels. Sometimes this is raised and called a *Churchill* rib, after the gunmaker EJ Churchill; or it might be a flat-file *Pigeon* rib or a sunken *Purdey*. The rib normally has a mat finish (to avoid reflection) as it is the sightline of the gun.

Round action – Where the lockwork is situated behind the receiver and mounted to the trigger-plate; making for a compact action which is rounded on the underside.

Self-opening guns – Guns that have a spring-assisted opening mechanism.

SG cartridges – Small game cartridges; usually loaded with 1oz of shot for pheasant, partridge and grouse and 1½ for wildfowl.

Side-by-side configuration – Double barrels so arranged.

Sidelock – See further development of firearms above.

Sleeved barrels – An economical method of replacing the bored part of worn out or damaged barrels. Cheaper guns are even often made with sleeved barrels, so that not all the metal in the barrels is of bore quality.

Stock – Wooden part of the gun at the shoulder end, as shown on the guns by Boss & Co in Plate 5.

Take-down – Type of rifle in which the barrel, the magazine and the stock may be dismantled for ease of travelling. Shotguns are always dismantled in their cases.

Trigger guard – Curved metal guard around the trigger[s].

Wrist – Thinnest part of the stock.

Modern gun-making

Just the same as bespoke clothes' makers, bespoke gunmakers will take measurements (usually around seven), such as lengths of arms to the joints; breadth of shoulders, and so on.

English walnut was acknowledged to be the best wood for gunstocks (stable and dense and well-figured) but there is little, if any, of it left – so now European walnut is used – such as that from the Dordogne and also from Turkey and, as with selecting briar wood for tobacco pipe-making, there are several different grades, depending (again), largely on the straightness and figure of the grain, and there are considerable differences in price.

With the bespoke option, you can opt for automatic or manual safety mechanisms as well as (detachable) droplocks; inter-changeable barrels of different bores and interchangeable chokes, as well as having the possibility of a single selective trigger. The type of game that you are after will influence various things, including triggers, and all this needs to be discussed with the gunmaker. For example, for grouse shooting, you will probably want a pair of shorter guns (for speed and manoeuvrability); whereas, for wildfowling pieces, you will probably want a longer over-and-under gun. There are choices in styles of engraving, (and chiseling) exterior metalwork; choices in different anti-recoil pads, and cases. Some makers can also offer guns *in the white* (a phrase originally applied to undyed cloth); that is to say, unfinished. This shortens the waiting time for fully bespoke guns but still allows for the making of correct stock sizes, personalized engraving and so forth and is broadly similar to better quality made-to-measure clothing; where you have to accept the basic pattern but can (within those limitations), have the article trimmed and fitted to correct size and other specifications for you. Some old makers, such as J Blanch & Son (one of the first makers to adopt the Lefaucheux pinfire breech-loading mechanism), sometimes used to build guns around actions made by Webley & Scott. J Blanch & Son still exist but trade in antique and secondhand guns. On a different note, some makers also still make guns explicitly in styles and using particular features developed by the great firms, such as Boss & Co, Holland & Holland and Purdey. Moreover, it has always been the case that piece workers are used in gunmaking (as in many bespoke services), and that not every piece of every gun that bears a particular maker's name has necessarily been made in-house. In some cases, as with the first guns from the firm that became Holland & Holland, whole guns have been made in the trade and then retailed under particular makers' names or supplied by other makers 'in the white' and finished in-house. The point is that, provided that the workmanship is up to 'Best' standard, this is perfectly acceptable and, of course, it is.

It takes between six hundred and fifty and twelve hundred and fifty hours of work to make a bespoke gun (sidelocks take longer than boxlocks and the differences in engraving can add much time too, from the normal rose and scroll; acanthus leaf patterns or oak, ivy or fern leaves, to more intricate arabesques or corombelle patterns; game scenes, stooping raptors, as well as heraldic devices or full achievements of arms or monograms, on 'escutcheons'), and remember that, in fully bespoke guns, even every pin (screw) is handmade. Moreover, you are often looking at a delivery period of around a year (compared with around three months for a pair of bespoke shoes or a couple of months for a bespoke suit).

Several gunmakers offer a variety of specialized services, such as: making their own Best Guns; selling and customizing good continental guns, such as Beretta and Aya; they sometimes act as brokers for used guns (their own and those made by other firms); they service, repair, renovate and restock guns and replace or sleeve barrels and they supply ammunition, cleaning sets, gun cases and gun-slips. Some of them (notably Holland & Holland), even sell clothing for use in the field.

The basic stages in building a gun are as follows. The barrel-maker brazes the barrels together, fits the ribs and joins the barrels to the action and the locking and cocking mechanisms. The extractors, lever work, bolts and spindles are fitted. Next the 'furniture' goes on; this comprises the trigger or triggers, trigger guard and the plates and the gun is smoothed off for engraving. The stocker makes the stock, which is 'made off' with a cast according to whether the gun is to be for a right or left-handed shot. The grip is hand-chequered and the engraving takes place, according to the customer's desires. Then the gun's barrels are colour-hardened (against rust) and then it is regulated, tested and proofed.

Something of a selection of a few of the best of many gunmakers

A A Brown
This firm, founded in 1930, which is still in business in Birmingham, has frequently made guns that have been retailed by other makers as their own. Besides their fine shotguns (the best of which is called the *Supreme De Luxe*), they are famous for the *Abas Major* compact air pistol and, during the Second World War, they made machine tools for the Spitfire fighter airplane.

Abbiatico & Salvinelli (Famars)
Founded in 1967, this fine Italian firm makes the most of modern technology and turns out Best Guns, in the style of Boss & Co, such as the Sovereign; not forgetting its impressive Africa Express double-barrelled rifle.

Arrieta y Cia
Founded eighty years ago by Avelino Arrieta, this Spanish firm makes fine bespoke guns, as well as supplying useful and popular guns off the shelf.

Asprey
Only in production between 1986 and 1997 (with a very few finished after that), these fine, bespoke shotguns certainly attracted their fans, including the Prince of Wales. Production of the same type and quality continues with William & Son: 'William' being William Asprey, now established in Mount Street.

Atkin, Grant & Lang
The first Henry Atkin was at James Purdey in 1814. His son, the second Henry Atkin, was apprenticed at Purdey and remained there for ten years before he went to William Moore & Co, then founding Henry Atkin in 1877. Atkin is

especially noted for making improvements to ejector mechanisms in shotguns. In 1960 this firm merged with Grant & Lang. Stephen Grant had been apprenticed in Dublin before he moved to Charles Lancaster and then Thomas Boss and, after Thomas Boss's death, he became the managing partner, before he set up on his own in 1867. Grant's sons joined in 1869 and it became Stephen Grant & Sons; eventually winning royal warrants across Europe and beyond. They took over Joseph Lang & Son in 1925 and other firms too, including Henry Atkin in 1960. After a short period of dormancy, the firm of Atkin, Grant & Lang opened its doors in Lincoln's Inn Fields. So far as the Lang side of it is concerned: in 1812, Joseph Lang worked for Alexander Wilson, establishing his own firm in 1821 in Haymarket and, in 1826, obtained all the stock of the bankrupt Joseph Manton. Lang also opened the first shooting gallery and school and played a major part in the development and adoption of breech-loading, pinfire guns.

Aya
This Spanish firm's off-the-shelf No 2 side by side is one of the most popular of the Spanish guns used in the UK.

Frederick Beesley
This firm was founded in 1880, after the founder had licensed the use of his spring-opening mechanism to his former employer, James Purdey. So innovative and skilled were the firm's makers that, in 1926, it secured the warrant of the then Prince of Wales (later Edward VIII and then Duke of Windsor). It specializes in fine handmade sidelocks but it also stocks foreign and secondhand guns, rifles and air-guns.

Beretta
The most famous Italian gun-maker, it was established in the early sixteenth century and, in 1526, supplied arms to the Arsenal of Venice. It remains in the control of the Beretta family and nowadays makes handguns, field guns (including express rifles) and even western style 'six shooters', as well as their famous over-and-under shotguns.

Boss & Co
Boss & Co can trace its origins to 1773, when William Boss began his apprenticeship in Birmingham. In the late eighteenth century he moved to Joseph Manton's firm in London and his son Thomas Boss was apprenticed to Manton. When Thomas finished his apprenticeship in 1812, he started his own firm in St James's Street, where he began making Best Guns only. This policy is still applied, prompting King George VI to say:

'A Boss gun, a Boss gun......bloody beautiful, but too bloody expensive!'

It is true to say that they are still, unashamedly, amongst the most expensive new guns in the world.

A Boss gun was such a favourite with Papa Hemingway that he used one *to end it all.*

The firm does, by popular demand, also make a more economical model, called the 'Robertson', named after John Robertson, who bought the firm in 1891 and devised the Boss single trigger in 1894, the Boss ejector in 1898 and their own over-and-under in 1909.

After a few moves around the West End, the shop and the workshop are now at Kew Bridge. A selection of shots of a fine pair of Boss & Co side-by-side shotguns is shown in Plate 6.

Browning

This American firm had its beginnings in John Browning's father's gun workshop in Ogden, Tennessee, when John first made a gun there, aged ten, in 1865. John Browning was a great innovator in many types of guns, including automatic weapons, such as the famous machine guns and semi-automatic weapons, such as the magazine pistols and the semi-automatic shotgun. He also made single shot guns and rifles as well as contributing to the famous Winchesters. The firm continues in the fine innovative tradition that he began. One of the favourite American guns is the *Superposed* over-and-under.

Charles Hellis

This firm was founded in 1884 in Westbourne Park. Charles Hellis had not received any formal apprenticeship in gunmaking. In 1897 the firm moved to Edgware Road and his sons joined it in 1902, moving to larger premises in 1935. They famously came to favour much shorter barrels than those of thirty inches (the general rule for shotguns) and started making them at twenty six- inches; which is a fast gun for grouse shooting, owing to the sudden appearance of fast birds. The firm closed in 1956 but the name was kept alive, if dormant, and eventually sold on to an owner who reopened the business.

Charles Lancaster

This firm (sometimes called 'The Gun House'), was founded in 1826 and has always been renowned for the excellence of its barrels.

Cogswell & Harrison

This is London's oldest surviving gunmaker, established in 1770 by Benjamin Cogswell, it became gun-maker to Prince Albert and now incorporates William

Moore & Grey, a firm that had its roots in William Moore's business founded in 1808 and later arose from an amalgamation between William Moore and William Parker Grey, both of whom had been employees of the great Joseph Manton. Its fine pieces are still sought after. Also subsumed in Cogswell & Harrison is another highly esteemed firm called Harrison & Hussey, which was founded in 1919.

E J Churchill
Established in 1891 and back in business after a period of dormancy, this famous gunmaker also has a shooting ground, where lessons and practice sessions may be had and an estate, where they stage 'corporate entertainment' and teach the bankers and other commercial boys which end is which of a shotgun; many of them would be far better engaged in spending more time getting the economy out of the mess that they have made of it but there we are.

Fabbri
This Italian firm makes the most of artisanal skills and the best of modern technology, firmly believing that all this can be melded together to make first rate guns.

Grulla Armas
This Spanish firm was established to make bespoke field guns (both shot guns and rifles), in 1932 and even offers a choice of engraving styles from Holland & Holland, to Purdey and Churchill.

Holland & Holland
This firm was founded in 1835, by Harris Holland, who was not a gunmaker at all but a tobacco wholesaler, with a passion for shooting. His first guns were made in the trade and just bore the name 'H Holland'. He probably started manufacturing guns in 1850 and, in 1861, his nephew, Henry Holland became an apprentice in the firm. When he completed his apprenticeship in1867, he became a junior partner and, from 1876, the firm assumed the name Holland & Holland. This firm's 'Royal' side-by-sides are world famous and keenly sought after. However, the firm's rifles have also been held in high regard since they won every category of *The Field* rifle trials in 1883.

J Purdey & Sons
In 1814, James Purdey, who had been a stocker at Joseph Manton, opened up on his own account and, in 1826, took over the old Manton premises in Oxford Street. His son assumed control in 1858 and the company followed the innovations of the age between the 1820s and 1890; from muzzle-loading

flintlocks of the 1820s to the breech-loading, hammerless ejectors of the 1880s, to which was added Frederick Beesley's self-opening mechanism, patented in 1890. The firm's first royal warrant was granted by the then Prince of Wales in 1868. In 1882 they moved to the corner of Mount Street and South Audley Street, taking in J Woodward & Son in 1949. Since 1994, they have been owned by the Richemont Group.

John Rigby & Co

As they say of themselves: '*Warranted by monarchs, borne by adventurers*' this firm, founded in Dublin in 1735, is famous for its superlative big game rifles but makes stalking rifles and fabulous shot guns too. It developed a London presence in 1865 and during the 1880s supervised the development of the legendary .303 military rifle at Enfield. Bearing in mind their reputation for dangerous big game guns, they maintain that every part of their guns '*…is made as though your life depends on it; as, indeed, it might*'. In 1900 they became the agents for Mauser and were behind the development of the Mauser magnum bolt action system, which they are still using. They make single shot stalking rifles, bolt action big game guns and double rifles as either sidelocks or boxlocks. The big game guns come in various calibres: .375 Holland & Holland; .416 Rigby; .450 Rigby; .458 Winchester; .458 Lott and the .500 Jeffrey. The firm's head office is now based in California but they have London agents in J. Roberts & Son.

John Wilkes

This firm was established in about 1830 and, although it no longer makes guns, repairs and servicing are still carried out by Craig Whitsey from premises in Arundel, West Sussex.

Joseph Brazier

Dating from 1827, this firm does still exist but it concentrates on making parts for other famous gunmakers.

Piotti

This Italian firm was founded by the Fratelli Piotti, Araldo and Faustino in the early 1960s and continues with the next generation.

Sauer & Sohn

This fine German company has been in business for over a century and, importantly, makes 'modular system' rifles, which can be used in different calibres, by substituting parts.

Schultz & Larsen

The firm, established in 1889 by Hans Schultz, makes very accurate sporting and target rifles and its UK distributor is VJC Supplies in Banbury, Oxfordshire.

Watson Bros

This firm was established in 1885 and has developed an especial reputation for small bore and lightweight guns, including over-and-unders.

Webley & Scott now Webley International

This is an iconic mass production British firearms' marque, tracing its roots back to 1790, becoming Webley & Son in 1834 and then, by merger with W & C Scott, Webley & Scott in 1857. They are again making shotguns, after a period during which they concentrated on their famous air guns (beloved of my generation) and one of their best current shotguns is an over-and-under sporting gun, called The Lichfield, after the late Patrick, Lord Lichfield, who was a Webley enthusiast. They no longer make their famous side-arms but what lustre attaches to the name: there is even a legend that before General George Armstrong Custer died at the Battle of Little Big Horn on 25 June 1876, he first emptied his pair of Webley & Scott double action revolvers at Sitting Bull's fellows. [A double-action revolver is one in which the trigger both fires the shot and *indexes* the revolving cartridge chamber to bring the next live round into alignment with the barrel to do so: the earliest revolvers were single-action in that the trigger just released the hammer to fire the round and the hammer had to be cocked manually and this action also revolved the chamber. However, since the guns were taken by the opposition, there is debate about this and they might have been Galand & Sommerville revolvers. Ned Kelly, the Australian outlaw, reputedly used Webley & Scott revolvers, that he had stolen from law enforcement officers. James A Garfield, the 20th President of the United States was tragically assassinated, by an unhinged speech-writer, using a .44 Webley & Scott British Bulldog revolver in September 1881. Their revolvers also featured in the Sherlock Holmes' stories; the James Bond adventures and in the television series *The Avengers*. For a long time Webley & Scott famously supplied the army and navy with side-arm revolvers. However, perhaps we should not leave this subject without noting that it was American Samuel Colt who actually invented the revolver ('The Great Equalizer') and even took out a British patent for it as early as 1835.

Westley Richards & Co

Established in 1812, by William Westley Richards, they are still making all types of sporting guns, including wonderful double rifles.

William & Son (from Asprey)

See under 'Asprey' above.

William Evans
Still at their splendid shop in St James's Street, this firm was established in 1883, and makes the full range of sporting guns.

W J Jeffrey & Co
Between 2000–2010, this firm's guns were actually made by **J Roberts & Son** which was founded in 1950 and it makes and supplies the complete range of best sporting guns (including big game and stalking guns) as well as being agents for the Spanish firm of **Arrizabalaga** and the Italian firm of **Battista Rizzini**.

William Powell & Sons
There had been an established Birmingham gun trade before the end of the seventeenth century, owing to the local abundance of minerals, including iron and these makers, over the years, satisfied the government's needs for firearms in the many armed conflicts that took place. The Powell family had been in Birmingham since the mid-seventeenth century and William Powell decided that it was time to upgrade the types of guns being produced and so he found the great gunmaker Joseph Simons and entered into partnership with him in 1802 in Birmingham High Street. Simons died and the firm moved to a building next to the Birmingham Proof House which had been established by the efforts of William Powell and other Birmingham gunmakers, in 1813; since when there has always been a Powell on the elected Board of Guardians. The firm exhibited at the Great Exhibition of 1851 and, concentrating on shotguns from the mid-nineteenth century, gathered up various patents for innovations in design: snap action (1864); half cocking lock (1866) and a 'loaded' indicator (1869). Between 1855 and 2008, the firm was in Carrs Lane but is now in Banbury. It has an association with the West Oxfordshire Shooting Ground.

Winchester
As influenced by the great John M Browning (who had made his first functioning gun at the age of ten years), this is still an iconic American marque; making a big range from shot guns to big game guns and, owing to the machine-production processes and less ornamentation, these fine guns come in at remarkably easy prices. This firm (along with Remington), is famous for its calibre numbers, such as the .243 and the .308.

WW Greener
Established in 1829, by William Greener and made famous by his son William Wellington Greener, this firm, is still making fine field guns under family direction.

Besides the above firms and, for the sake of reasonable completeness, there are also the following other firms: **AA Brown & Sons** (1938, Birmingham);

Anderson Wheeler; **Bozard & Co** (originally established in 1888, London; dormant for long and now in the active ownership of Philip Turner, formerly of Purdey and Holland & Holland); **Du Moulin Herstal SA** (Liège); **JR Dickinson & Son** (1820, Edinburgh); **Merkel** (1898, in Suhl – 'the German Damascus'); **Verney-Carron** (1820, St Etienne, France);

Shotgun maintenance and cleaning

You must remember that, just like anything else that has working parts, your guns will need regular cleaning and maintenance and you need a kit that will include rods and brushes, suitable to the bore of your guns, a toothbrush, bore solvent, lintless cloths and gun oil. It is best that you ask a gunmaker to demonstrate to you how to dismantle and clean and then reassemble a gun.

Gun and game licences

You need a shotgun licence to possess shotguns (in Northern Ireland it is called a firearms' licence) and the system for firearms, covering rifles in the rest of the UK, is similar. The application form is available from the local police station and gun possession is subject to rigorous control, including over the storage of guns and ammunition. You will need to fill in an application form, that requires you to state essential personal details and disclose any criminal convictions and any medical conditions that could affect ownership and use of firearms (medical conditions may be checked with your doctor). You will also be asked about gun storage and need to know about the safety requirements for gun cabinets. The form must be counter-signed by a person of standing, who has known you for two years and you must send in four passport photographs too. You will be visited by an officer to assess you and the security of your housing. If the licence is refused, there is an appeal system against the refusal and you would be as well to seek legal advice on this, if necessary. Possession of a criminal record or certain medical conditions can present obstacles to the grant of a licence.

Before you go shooting game, make sure that your activities are also covered by any necessary game licence (available from the Post Office) or an exemption from the need for it (apart from wildfowl licences for geese, under the Wildlife Act 1990, this now applies only in Scotland and Northern Ireland in the UK), and that the game that you are after is in season and that you are not going out 'after hours' or on a day when it is prohibited (see below).

Storing guns and ammunition

It is a condition of the grant of a gun licence in the UK that you have secure storage for your guns and always store guns and ammunition separately. Special safety cabinets must meet (at least) minimum security standards and are made by specialist companies (such as Brattonsound), and cabinets should be bolted to the wall (maybe inside a cupboard).

Secondhand sporting guns

Several of the makers, mentioned above, also sell secondhand sporting guns, as well as their own bespoke and off the shelf new stock and besides the auctioneers mentioned in relation to duelling pistols, on page 14, Gavin Gardiner also holds auctions of fine sporting guns made between 1860 and the present. When choosing your guns, remember that it is far better to have one really good gun than several mediocre ones.

Examples of shooting grounds and schools

If you are seeking instruction in gun-handling and shooting, there are places such as: the Institute of Clay Shooting Instructors; the Holland & Holland Shooting Ground, and The West London Shooting School. There are, additionally, many clay shooting grounds throughout the country and, indeed, abroad, listed in the telephone directories.

The driven shoot

The best driven shoots yield high, fast birds. These are often run by syndicates, which lease the gaming rights over estates and arrange the rearing of birds for release, lay on the keeper, the beaters and the pickers-up and dogs. Examples of open syndicate places (and prices) may be viewed on sites such as shooting4all.com. They do not usually provide guns. There are also still some private estates where shooting can be had for a few days at fixed prices. Examples are Belvoir and the Glenstriven Estate, Argyll, Scotland and then there are also hotels that arrange fishing and shooting. An example of one of these is Bracken Bank Lodge, Cumbria. There are also specialist sporting agencies, such as Davis & Bowring, which arrange the purchase of sporting days all over the world. Shooting is now a sport indulged in by a diverse cross-section, including not just the usual suspects, but also: bankers, rockers, dockers, drummers, songsters, film stars, footballers and their managers, and many similar types, most of whom probably need to be told which end to point up in the air. But at least they have the cash to keep the sport alive.

Safety of all concerned is the golden rule when shooting; so never point a gun (whether loaded or not) at anyone. Keep it loaded only when it is to be used and, before use, point it at the ground. Never swing the gun over the heads of any line of guns (in this context 'guns' means 'people') or fire it anywhere that you cannot see, such as into coverts (silent 't'), meaning copses and overgrowth.

Some things are, by convention, not shot: infrequently hen pheasants are spared; white pheasants (maybe out of superstition as well as because they are highly visible and help to identify where the birds are moving); a hare in her form; keepers and beaters (no matter how bad the sport); and winging and 'tailoring' game (blasting its rear off) is shoddy. Firing at low-flying birds is frowned on as bad sportsmanship and also results in spoiled food. It is actually (subject to small exceptions), illegal to shoot game at night, on Sundays and on Christmas Day (in Scotland observance of Sunday and Christmas Day is by convention and not by law), as well as out of the seasons that are regulated by the Game Act 1831, the Wildlife and Countryside Act 1981, and the Deer Act 1991, read with the Wildlife Act 1990. Some birds, such as the endangered Capercaillie are subject to voluntary bans on Crown Estate land (even if they cannot preserve Jermyn Street, they are good for something); certain private estates and land owned by the Royal Society for the Protection of Birds. Some birds, such as the white-fronted goose are subject to general voluntary bans amongst wildfowlers.

There have been introductions of certain game birds into Britain; most importantly pheasants, by the Romans (who introduced them to Europe generally) and then more again by the Normans and, less significantly (as it is a runner rather than a flier), the French or red-legged partridge, (*Alectoris rufa*), in the reign of Charles II. There are several different varieties of pheasant both wild and bred to shoot; principally the common pheasant (*Phasianus colchicus*) and the variant, the ring-necked pheasant as well as hybrids. Wild pheasants fly higher and faster (and therefore make better sport), than the semi-domesticated types. They are also tougher to eat and need to be hung for longer.

For driven pheasant and partridge (driven by a line of walking beaters tapping the ground), unless you are put to be the 'rear-ender', walking gun to walk behind the beaters and pick off birds that fly in the opposite direction of the drive, you'll have a numbered standing 'peg' (they are in a line, between twenty and forty yards apart and you draw lots for the first allocation of them). Pheasants come in 'drives' or, if many together, 'flushes' (on the ground, a group is a 'nye'); partridge come in 'drives' or 'coveys' (they also roost in 'coveys' on the ground, facing outwards in a circle to detect danger).

For grouse, you will have a 'butt' (a low-hedged standing area); grouse also come in 'drives' and grouse moors are often called 'hills'. Pegs and butts are situated to maximise the chances that the birds will reach a good height and speed as they are driven down over the guns.

Keep to the peg or butt allotted to you (there may be eight or nine pegs; often fewer butts) and, if you are close to other pegs, imagine that there are swimming lanes overhead, marking the safe arc of fire and to ensure that you do not take your neighbours' birds (unless they miss them). Shoot high birds but do not try to shoot birds that you believe that you will miss or merely maim.

If you are unfortunate enough to injure any person, you must leave the shoot at once. Normally, discretion in relation to these incidents is observed but, if you injure someone badly then, apart from any legal consequences, you will be expected never to be seen on a shoot again. Recklessness or negligence (as well as specific intent to injure) in shooting legally takes the matter of any resulting human injury outside the ambit of mere accident and could have serious criminal consequences as well as resulting in a civil action for damages for personal injury.

The point at which driven shooting may start and must end may be marked by a blast on a horn or a whistle. At the end of a drive the keeper will call "All out!" At this point, for pheasant and partridge drives, the guns move to the next stand of pegs, for the second drive and often each gun moves up two places (to ensure that everyone gets some good sport) and this may be repeated for up to six or seven drives a day (but, in practice, there are seldom more than five). The same goes for movement between butts. The number of drives will often be limited, on commercial and syndicate shoots, by reference to the intended bag and once that bag figure has been reached, shooting stops.

So far as bringing dogs and cross country vehicles are concerned, it is best to notify the host that you are bringing these in advance and remember to take a ground peg to tether the dog.

Once they are dead, birds are gathered as follows: pheasant are gathered singly (although often people speak of a 'brace' of pheasant and they are tied two together); grouse and partridge are gathered in 'brace' (twos); quail are counted in 'couples' and, apart from exceptions, mentioned below, most other species are gathered and counted singly.

Obviously, to achieve any reasonable success, you need a decent gun; once it would have been a loader and at least one pair of decent guns. Three guns and two loaders might be preferable for a top shot but a novice is going to be mercilessly ribbed for having more than a pair of guns in use at any one time. There will be pickers-up and retrievers but it is the responsibility of each gun to mark where his own quarry falls. Guns will be told whether serendipitous ground game may also be taken (often it may not, as it could endanger the pickers-up) and whether only cock pheasants. Whatever you have paid for your shooting and however impressive your 'bag', you are going to walk away only with a brace of birds; the rest go to the other guns a brace a piece; the same for the keeper and beaters and pickers-up and the game dealers take the rest to be sold to contribute to the expenses for the next year's sport.

Thank the head keeper at the end and tip him, at current rates, around twenty pounds for a bag of up to one hundred and fifty pheasant and for between one hundred and fifty and two hundred and fifty, around thirty pounds and so on. The same goes for any hired loader. For grouse shooting, the amounts will vary according to the invitation and whether you are a paying guest. Remember, for grouse shooting, to take your *unloaded* guns to and fro' the butts in gun slips.

Walked-up or 'rough' shooting

This can be great fun and is often to be enjoyed on one's own land or on that of friends. It just means going out with gun dogs (probably spaniels or pointers), spreading out in a line to walk the game up and picking off whatever seasonable game, rabbits or pigeons (these last two are not actually game) that you walk-up. Airborne snipe come in groups, called 'walks' or 'wisps' and woodcock come in 'falls'. These are not strictly game either (at least not defined as such by statute). Bags of shot snipe or woodcock are counted in 'couples'. Woodcock, rising up, suddenly and vertically, with great speed, are amongst the most challenging birds to shoot. There is even an exclusive (but meritocratic) club, called *The Shooting Times' Woodcock Club*, for guns who have been witnessed shooting a couple of woodcock with 'a right and a left', without lowering the gun.

This kind of shooting is a relaxed and relaxing way to enjoy some sport, as well as the least expensive shooting to be had and often results in something for everyone's pot. Just remember to bear in mind how many men and dogs are in your party and be aware of where they are at all times so that you do not shoot over them. Also take care to ensure that you do not shoot over or near any highway or footpath and remember that, even where there are no footpaths, there might be trespassers or adventurous children; therefore, again do not shoot into any area that you cannot clearly see is free of humans, dogs, farm animals and other wildlife and walk with your gun (preferably broken), pointing at the ground. Moreover, if you are on someone else's land and there are crops under foot, be sure that you do not trample them; close gates that are supposed to be closed; if you are forced to climb a gate, put your gun on the ground and climb over the hinge side of the gate (if you climb the latch side, the leverage will weaken the hinges). Do not (especially with a gun), scramble through prickly coverts and over hedges. Douglas Sutherland in his amusing book, *The English Gentleman*, mentions a nice little rhyme in relation to gun safety:

> Never, never let your gun
> Pointed be at anyone...
> All the pheasants ever bred
> Will not make up for one man dead.

As with wildfowling, when shooting walked-up game, quarry identification is important as it is both illegal and thoroughly irresponsible to shoot protected species or game out of season.

Wildfowling

These are two methods of wildfowling; the first is on estuaries with dogs and the other is to lie in wait at flight pounds. This is subject to a general licensing system, under the Wildlife Act 1990, in respect of geese, with which all participants should acquaint themselves. There is also power, under the Wildlife and Countryside Act 1981, to make (from time to time), Orders by Statutory Instrument proscribing the hunting of specified species of wildfowl in periods of severe weather and every wildfowler should inquire into this (through the relevant Government Department responsible for environmental matters), before setting out. The British Association For Shooting And Conservation ('AFSAC') and the Countryside Alliance also keep track of this legislation.

The specific and current details are available through their websites, as well as information about organized wildfowling, which is the only way of undertaking foreshore wildfowling. Remember also that, for environmental protection, lead shot is banned over wetland areas. The ability to make reliable quarry identification is very important, as only certain species of waterfowl may be shot and current specifications are available on the AFSAC website. Canada geese are regarded as pests and subject to general licence (from time to time), under the Wildlife Act 1990, for year-round culling.

Airborne geese come in groups called 'skeins'; duck come in 'flights'. Shot mallard duck can be counted in 'brace' or 'pairs'; teal may be counted in 'pairs' or 'couples'. The rest (including widgeon), are counted singly. Useful dogs to pick them up are Irish water spaniels.

Great shots

Two of the greatest game-shots straddling the Nineteenth and Twentieth Centuries are consistently said to have been Lord Ripon (born Earl de Grey) (1852–1923) and Lord Walsingham (1843–1919). Earl de Grey succeeded to become the second Marquis of Ripon in 1909. His lifetime bag comprised 556,813 head of game and, thanks to his use of three guns and fast loaders, it was not unknown for him to have had up to *seven dead birds in the air at the same time*. Aged seventy-one, on 22 September 1923, at 3.15 pm, having just despatched fifty-one grouse in a drive and as they were being picked up, he dropped dead on the hill: what a way to go! Lord Ripon probably takes the trophy as the greatest game shot of all time and his record, made during England's Golden Age for country sport, is now unlikely to be surpassed.

One remarkable single feat from these times that deserves mention was that of Captain Horatio Ross (1801–1886), a celebrated sportsman and all round shot, who shot eighty-two grouse, with eighty two shots, on his eighty-second birthday. For those interested in more about record bags and unusual shooting, I recommend Hugh S Gladstone's book, mentioned in the Bibliography.

Double shots

Apart from bringing down two or more birds of the same species with one shot, a double shot is also getting two different *species* with one shot. Some recorded examples, from *The Field* magazine are: a snipe and a thrush; a partridge and a hare; a pheasant and two rabbits; a snipe and a grouse; a hare and a quail and a rabbit and a woodcock. There is even an example of a hare and a salmon, mentioned in a report in The *Daily Mail* for 29 July 1921, relating to a single shot, in Connemara, Ireland, in August 1886, at a grouse shoot by William O'Malley MP, who actually shot a hare (that he had not seen) and also a ten pound salmon jumping in a river beyond! He seems to have missed the grouse.

Dress and refreshments

The most fortunate people go to shoot, on their own land or the land of their friends. There you will find many of them in their badges of honourable experience: fully seasoned, weathered tweeds (including unlined plus twos), over silk long johns, viyella shirts, old (probably skew-whiff) ties and caps or battered felt hats; shooting stockings; deeply-dubbined field boots or shoes and gaiters and Schoffel and Barbour coats. Apart from the tailors and other makers mentioned in *History of Men's Fashion*, there is a good supplier of men's country and sporting wear called Bookster at tweed-jacket.com but make sure that you have plus twos for shooting and not knee breeches unless they are of the moleskin variety for wearing on very rough days. The other good general supplier of clothing for country sports is, of course, Cording's of Piccadilly. As already mentioned, Holland & Holland supply a good range of sporting dress, as well as fine guns and then there is also Anderson Wheeler. You should also really wear ear plugs or other protectors; certainly for any prolonged period of potting away and the gunmakers sell them.

Your tweeds might well be Donegal (maybe by John Molloy), or Harris tweed (from the independent weavers and available through the cloth houses and tailors or W Bill. If you are fortunate enough to have your own Scottish estate, you will be wearing your own estate tweeds from Johnston's of Elgin.

So far as vents on coats are concerned: equestrian coats and jackets have to have a single central back vent and shooting jackets often have action backs too – with vents at the shoulders or a vertical, pleated and lapped dorsal vent.

Originally, the informally intentioned lounge suit coats had no vents. After the Second World War and under the influence both of Neil Munro 'Bunny' Roger (exponent of the New Edwardian style, adapted for the character of John Steed in the 1960s-1970s' television series *The Avengers*, and later exaggerated by the Teddy Boys – and continued, to some extent by Ozwald Boateng), *and* exponents of the sleeker 'Conduit cut', such as Anthony Sinclair, tailor to Sean Connery's screen James Bond, vents started becoming more prevalent in ordinary lounge suits. They had existed before; for example, the Duke of Windsor (as Prince of Wales) had double vents on a 1929 Frederick Scholte suit coat. However, Cary Grant's famous grey checked suit in the 1959 film *North by Northwest* did not have any vents. In this film Grant plays beleaguered Roger O Thornhill, innocently caught up in espionage and murder:

> 'What does the 'O' stand for?'
> 'Nothing.'

In chapter 8 of the 1963 James Bond novel *On Her Majesty's Secret Service*, Fleming has Bond mock a suit coat (which he has made to impersonate the baronet Sir Hilary Bray, in his mission to track Blofeld), because it has *double* vents at the back, with the words '…quite the little baronet..'

Seasoned sportsmen carry beaten, creased and stained old cartridge bags, dented flasks and scratched cake tins, containing sandwiches or pasties; Kendal mint cake and chocolate. They might have thermos flasks, containing Bovril, bouillon or consommé, enlivened with sherry or spirit; a trendy version of this is called 'Bullshot' and combines a hot consommé with vodka, Tabasco and Worcester sauces, lime juice, black pepper and celery salt, all according to taste. A hip flask might contain 'The King's Ginger'; a warming liqueur which Berry Bros & Rudd formulated for King Edward VII in 1903. Shooting sticks are a great convenience as are cartridge belts and remember to use a proper game book and record all your kills.

More likely than not, these people use their grandfathers' guns; since nearly the only people that can afford a pair of bespoke Best London guns now are the pointless (and often clueless) 'celebrities' of the modern age. For some people, £100,000 is a meaningful fraction of a retirement sum; for these 'celebrity' guys and gals it might be anything from just a medium-sized luncheon party to a pair of guns. There is even one 'celebrity' couple who charge 'nobody' strangers £100,000 for the mutual embarrassment of spending the evening with them. I know of one eccentric fellow who paid them and then deliberately stood them up. These celebrities' often pointless 'occupations' and their mindless popularity and astronomical pay comprise one of the reasons why the remains of western civilization are slipping into the abyss. Moreover, it is difficult not to recall that the charity *Wateraid* could buy and install 500 rope-pump wells in desert places with £100,000; each benefitting a whole community of beleaguered humanity.

Sporting guns are, normally, side-by-side double barrelled shotguns in 12 bore or (as already mentioned), especially for the ladies and youngsters, the lighter 20 bore and the .410 gauge. There are also guns in 16, 20 and 28 bore. If you use over-and-under guns for game-birds, you might want a bore smaller than 12 because these guns are a little heavier than side-by-sides. Especially if you are not a *paying* guest on a shoot, besides tipping, as suggested above, write a note to thank the host for the day's sport.

Gundogs and gundog training

Joining the Gundog Club is a good place to start with this but the detail of gundog training is beyond the scope of this book.

Shooting seasons

The open seasons for game are, except where otherwise stated, for England and Wales and are as set out below. Much more detailed information for the United Kingdom (including any up-to-date Orders and General Licences) are available from the website of The British Association for Shooting and Conservation (basc.org.uk). The purpose of close seasons is to enable successful breeding and rearing of young and any movements between breeding and wintering grounds. For pheasant the open season is between 1 October and 1 February; for partridge between 1 September and 1 February; for wildfowl (inland) between 1 September and 31 January; (below High Water Mark) it is between 1 September and 20 February; for grouse (Scotland) between 12 August (the 'Glorious 12th') and 10 December; for Ptarmigan (Scotland) between 12 August and 10 December; for common snipe (jack snipe being protected) between 12 August and 31 January; for woodcock between 1 October and 31 January; for blackgame between 20 August and 10 December; for golden plover between

1 September and 31 January. The close season for hare is between 1 March ('mad as a March hare') and 31 July. Woodpigeon and rabbits are not game but pigeon shooting is subject to a general licence under the Wildlife Act 1990, for the purpose of protecting crops and rabbits do, under old legislation, enjoy a close season on moorland and unenclosed land and may be shot there only between 1 September and 31 March. Before undertaking this pursuit, you should acquaint yourself with the current law, including the terms of general licences, for the place in question.

For stalking deer (here described in Scotland only) the seasons are, for red deer: stags between 1 July and 20 October; the hinds are stalked between 21 October and 15 February; fallow bucks are stalked between 1 August and 30 April; the does are stalked between 21 October and 15 February; roe bucks are stalked between 1 April and 20 October and the does between 21 October and 31 March. Before undertaking any of these pursuits, you should acquaint yourself with the current law, including licences, for the place in question.

Deer stalking and big game hunting

Stalking deer (or bigger or more dangerous game, come to that) is a combined art and science that cannot be learned from books and there are various organizations which offer courses in everything from stalking and marksmanship to compliance with health and safety regulations concerning assessment of carcasses (bearing in mind that game often enters the human food chain) and dealing with carcasses – 'gralloching' is the practice of gutting at the scene of the kill. One such is The British Deer Society and these are also the St. Hubert Club and Red Deer Outdoors. Simondeum offers hunting safari packages in Namibia. Legendary Adventures offer the same in Tanzania. So far as deer stalking is concerned: there is hill stalking for red deer and woodland stalking, for roe and fallow deer. Expanding, soft bullets are used and a popular calibre is the .308 Winchester, using 190 grain bullets. 7mm Steyr Mannlicher rifles are also popular.

Field glasses-binoculars

Here there are several excellent makes. In the specification of the power, the first figure is the unit of magnification and the second figure is the diameter in millimeters of the objective lens. Examples are: Leica 12X50 and the 10X25 (Compact); Bushnell 7X26 Compact; Canon 18X50 IS; Carl Zeiss 8X30 Conquest, and the Nikon 8X30 and the 10X35 E2.

The powerful, modern compact binoculars may easily be used in the field, at the theatre and opera and at the races, as well as for bird watching or even spying on your neighbours.

Something of sport and morality

Prehistoric man hunted wild animals, out of plain necessity, with wood and flint spears. The Egyptians and other ancients threw relays of sticks at game birds and some used slings, falcons and hawks, dogs, traps or nets to catch all kinds of game. Then came longbows, crossbows and, eventually, guns. The earliest British game-keepers were employed to harvest their Masters' game as food as much as to guard it (along with the doves kept in columbaria and edible coarse fish and trout in stew ponds), before shooting became a sport at all and game has, for millennia, been regarded as an important basic source of food for mankind. In certain primitive societies it remains so.

Modern objection is taken to the continuance of the practice of hunting, with guns, because such game-hunting is said to be no longer a necessity and tales of the amazing slaughter of thousands of pheasants, shot for sport, and then (allegedly) ultimately left to rot, in the late nineteenth and early twentieth century, live on, as well as hard facts, such as the regrettable driving to extinction of certain species, including the Great Bustard and (but for its re-introduction from Sweden), the Capercaillie. A project is currently underway to introduce the Great Bustard into the Wiltshire countryside, with the first chicks hatched in May 2009. However, all this adds fuel to the fire of opposition to game-hunting as sport (which opposition, surely, is often founded on mere contrariness); as do facts such as the continuing need to protect the Jack Snipe; or magnificent raptors, such as the Peregrine Falcon and Osprey, that were routinely shot and poisoned by the game-keepers and ghillies of estates to protect (respectively) their pheasants, reared by hand, for release as sport and their rivers' salmon.

On top of all this, there are the 'right-on', urban, chattering classes ('the Urbanites') who harbour chippy, ill-considered prejudices, culminating in the unthinking insistence that the remaining, hearty pleasures of stubbornly surviving countrymen should be spoiled by adding bans on shooting and fishing to the foxhunting 'ban', with further cries of *à la lanterne*! for so much that they recklessly misunderstand.

The Urbanites' point of view is all held regardless of the facts that: owners of estates that provide shooting are very careful to preserve the natural habitats enjoyed not just by game birds but by much wildlife; shot game in the United Kingdom nowadays is either consumed by those involved in the chase or sold and, for the initiated, its availability adds considerably to the variety of 'organically produced' meats for consumption, including: black grouse; red grouse; ptarmigan; partridge; pheasant; woodcock; snipe; all the variety of wildfowl, from mallard, to teal and widgeon and geese; as well as ground game:

hare and deer. None of these creatures ever suffers the constriction of movement that the Urbanites overlook when they tuck in to their *cotoletta alla Milanese* in their mock-Italian *trattoria*.

Moreover, in the countryside, as indeed with fox-hunting, it is not, actually, just the likes of elderly Baronets and belted Earls who engage in the sport of game shooting but a cross-section of countrymen who are, often, to some extent, engaged in providing the meat, vegetables, fruit, bread and milk which (nicely slaughtered, skinned, gutted and cleaned; scraped, peeled, de-cored, refined and homogenized, as necessary), the squeamish Urbanites so greedily and carelessly buy in their 'supermarkets'.

In these 'supermarkets', the washed, bland, greyish meat goods appear in sealed, plastic and foam covers in regular, bite-size pieces (as though the whole process of production had taken place in a factory where no copulation; breath of life; bloodied, birthing eggs; afterbirth; existence; apprehension; death blows; broken bones; plucked feathers or stripped skins, and spilled guts had ever had any part at all). Otherwise the Urbanites consume these goods in their boutique brasseries and this means that they never even see the meat raw.

Given that the days (if they really existed), of slaughter beyond usefulness of game birds has long gone, if there is any moral argument in play here, maybe it is this: that those who cannot bear the thought of killing a creature and then appropriately stripping and cleaning it, before cooking it should:

(1) properly become vegetarians, or
(2) at least have the good grace to cease to rail against the sporting activities of those who contribute to the carnivore-centred, urban gastronomy that the Urbanites are enabled, with such thoughtful sensitivity, to enjoy.

I would say to the Urbanites: 'Put That in Your Pipe and Smoke It' but, of course, these Urbanites don't smoke.

The recent proliferation of Farmers' Markets has done something to redress these prejudices, bringing properly hung game into the food chain in the heart of our towns and cities.

One way to ensure that field sports are not banned is to have regard for the traditions of: respect for the creatures being hunted (and their habitats) and, indeed, all creatures at large; to have paramount regard for the safety of all the people involved and to show them courtesy. To this one might add, as slightly lesser considerations: be correctly (and not too carefully and *newly*) dressed and do not shoot beyond your ability to hit and kill the target.

It is interesting to note how many expressions in general use derive from hunting: 'bowled over' and ' brought to book' all refer to the killing of the quarry by hounds and are otherwise metaphors, respectively, for 'astonished' and 'brought to account'; to 'draw a blank' is to fail to flush the quarry from coverts. Moreover, there are expressions too that relate to fair play and sportsmanship: a fox is 'given law' when he is allowed a fair chance after being flushed out and before the hounds go into 'full cry' after him. If he outwits the hounds for long enough or crosses into another hunt's territory, he might, in the Master's discretion, be 'given best' and so be pursued no more that day.

Pest control

In relation to Taliban terrorist control: there are two methods, the first is to walk them up over pointers and the second, faster, method is to drive them and pick them off, in couples, as they flood overhead. Those in burkas are in the same position as hen pheasants (on a no-hens day), and immune from being shot; regardless of any suspicion that they are male terrorists in ignoble disguise.

For Somali pirate control, there is one most effective method, which is, from a suitable hide, to watch the arrival of the skein of pirates in the marshes at dusk, and then, as they descend, have six to eight crack-shot guns blast away at them with eight bores and either a Henry Nock blunderbuss, inscribed around the muzzle with the legend '*Fly or Die*' or a boat-mounted, six bore punt gun (which is a massive shotgun that is too heavy to hold). Send out Irish water spaniels to pick them up.

CHAPTER 2

Country and Sea Sports – Game Fishing

Man's life is but vain;
For 'tis subject to pain,
And sorrow, and short as a buble;
'Tis a hodge podge of business,
And mony, and care;
And care, and mony, and trouble.
But we'll take no care
When the weather is fair,
Nor will we vex though it rain;
We'll banish all sorrow,
And sing till tomorrow,
And Angle, and Angle again.

The Angler's Song, from *The Compleat Angler*, by Izaak Walton

Introduction

Many ancient people fished with rods that came to be called 'angles' in medieval England. There are a few main types of angling: first, fly-fishing for freshwater game fish (salmon (*Salmonidae* family) trout, and, char (both in the sub-family *Salmoninae*). Then there is coarse fishing, in one of several ways (including, sometimes: with flies; with floats; legering with weights, and spinning bait), for fish such as grayling; chubb; barbel; bream; carp; dace; ide; perch; pike; roach; rudd; tench; wels catfish, and zander. There is sea and lake or loch fishing from shore or in boats and there is deep sea big game fishing, for exotics such as blue marlin. I concentrate in this section on game fishing of both the kinds that I have mentioned. Accordingly, I have not given the scientific names for coarse fish.

Izaak Walton (1593–1683), from whose work the quotation comes at the beginning of this section, was a linen draper and sempster in Chancery Lane, London and a member of the Ironmongers' Company, which covered his trade.

He was also an ardent angler. His most enduring publication is *The Compleat Angler* (1653); which is written in an aphoristic, dialogue style, between (after revision): Piscator (the fisherman), Venator (the hunter) and Auceps (the falconer). Walton also wrote well-received biographies of various eminent men of the age, including his friend, the great metaphysical poet and divine Dr John Donne, Dean of St Paul's Cathedral, and is thus often said to be the father of modern biography. Of Donne's last moments, he wrote: 'He closed his own eyes; and then disposed his hands and body into such a posture as required not the least alteration by those that came to shroud him.' *The Lives*, mentioned in the Bibliography is certainly entrancing reading, as is *The Compleat Angler*.

There are two main types of trout fishing: first there is fishing in chalk streams, such as the River Test, and this is dry fly fishing, with a floating line; cast on the rise as the fish feed, or cast upstream on the water. Secondly, there is fishing in acid waters, when wet flies are used on a slow-sinking line, which is cast across the waters.

Rods and lines

Although no one is going to be much of an angler without a good line, obviously a decent rod is going to be the first purchase. Here it is necessary to consider where the rod is to be used and for what fish. This is because the environment and the type of fish to be caught will influence the choice of the most appropriate rod, according to whether you are going into deeper water in waders after salmon or fishing for trout in shallower water, which is surrounded by trees and bushes. Rods may be generally classified by their *weight*, *length* and *action*. Similarly, since flies (including nymphs) are light, weight is needed in the line, to get the right momentum, according to the distance to be cast and the type of fish that you are after. Two to four weights are for small fish and short casts. Five and six weights are good general purpose lines and weight seven (and up) is for salmon and for bigger fish.

Single-handed fly rods normally come at lengths between seven and ten feet and each is of one of three 'action' types. A slow action rod bends towards the handle end of the rod; a medium action rod bends in the middle and a fast action rod bends at the distal end and is designed to achieve the greatest reach. The most sought-after rods are still nowadays split cane, as described below; although graphite and glass rods are also performance rods. The line used, besides conforming to one of the standard weights and diameters (with corresponding breaking points in terms of pounds of load) will best be made of plastic and will be one of five main kinds: taper: this tapers away from the reel end; double-taper: this tapers away both towards the reel end and away from it (meaning that you can reverse a damaged double-taper line if the hook end is damaged); weight-forward: this tapers out towards the hook end; level: is a line that does not taper at all, and triangle taper: this is a gradual taper a way that becomes a level line.

The *leader* is a piece of line, made of nylon or fluorocarbon and is transparent in water and is attached to the main line and then either tied to the fly or to another piece of line, called a *tippet*, a uniform diameter material tied to the leader at one end and the fly at the other. The advantage of using a tippet is that every time you cut a fly off to replace it, you reduce the tippet and not the leader.

Reels

The very best reels are made of machined bar stock and the cheaper versions are formed or pressed. Reels have an *arbour*, which is the inner cylinder around which the line is wound. The larger the arbour, the more the control can be exercised over the line. *Backing* goes onto the reel first to bulk it up and act as extra line if a fish pulls the main line out from the reel.

Flies

'Flies' are artificial lures (suggestive of food) to get the fish onto the hook. Lures come as three types: dry flies, which represent the adult stage of insects, floating on the surface of the water. Then there are wet flies, such as nymphs, which represent the larva stage of insect development and are submerged. Nymphs constitute the greatest part of fish food. Then there are streamers too, which imitate small fish or leeches (streamers are really meant for lake or reservoir fishing). All flies are tied, which is a considerable art in itself. Selecting appropriate flies to use for any particular time of year and location will depend on the local insect population and their life cycles.

Some makers and suppliers

World-famous Hardy Brothers (now Hardy & Grey's), was originally founded in 1872 by William Hardy, who started out as a gunsmith at Alnwick, where the company's headquarters remain. He was joined by his brother John James and, following their favourite hobby, they turned their attention to making fishing rods and equipment. The woods used in the early nineteenth century for making fishing rods had included such as hickory, because they are supple and resilient, but by 1880 bamboo started to come to the forefront of attention and the Hardy Brothers decided to use split cane. The rods are made of Tonkin bamboo cane (*Arundinaria amabilis*), a species which grows only along a stretch of the River Sui, in the Guangdong Province of China. Only A-grade culms (lengths) are used, to be tempered over flame and then split, before the pieces are glued together to make these superlative rods. In fact only first rate materials are ever used in the making, including champagne grade cork shives from the cork oaks of Portugal and Spain and olive wood for the reel seats and ferrule stoppers. Their split cane Palakona rod won a gold medal at an early international exhibition. In 1891 they started marketing the Hardy Perfect Reel and were the first rod-maker to offer bridge rings, spiral lock-fast joints, stud-lock joints, split-end joints 'W' and screw-grip fittings. They also introduced the ingenious ball-bearing reels and were the first with a check mechanism in the reel arbour. They have acquired ten royal warrants and have recently acquired the firms of Grey's and Chub Fishing. Going from strength to strength, the Hardy GEM saltwater rod has recently won international acclaim.

The firm of Edward Barder is also the maker of amongst the finest split cane fly and coarse fishing rods in the world. Edward Barder trained at Hardy's in Pall Mall and, by 1990, he was established at a mill in Berkshire, on his own account.

Chris Lythe, who undertook five-and-a-half years' apprenticeship with machine company Rose Forgrove Ltd, makes various centre pin reels and is acknowledged as one of the best makers around.

Another fine firm, for fly rods, reels and the other equipment is Charles Clemes, under the ownership of Anderson Wheeler.

Farlow's of Pall Mall are great stockists of various makers' fishing equipment: including Hardy and Tibor reels and Hardy, Loomis, Sage and Orvis rods.

The Ferraris and Lamborghinis of fly fishing equipment are represented by companies such as G Loomis and Sage, which are companies based in the USA manufacturing a big range of fishing equipment. The Donegal Fly Company (based in Ireland), manufactures high quality flies. Of course, there are books on tying your own flies, if you have the time and one of the best known is by Helen Shaw and mentioned in the Bibliography.

Knots

Knots on the backing, line, leader and tippet are needed for obvious reasons. Those in most use are: the *arbour* knot to attach the backing to the line; the *clinch* to attach the fly to the leader or the tippet (as the case may be); the *nail* to attach the leader to the fly line, and the *surgeon's* to join the leader and tippet. Unless you know them already, you need to have an experienced fisherman demonstrate these knots to you and then practise them.

Casting

There are two basic methods of casting fly lines: there's the *overhead* and the *roll*. The overhead is the traditional method but is difficult to perform in areas with close bankside bushes and trees and the roll is the alternative, which is particularly effective with graphite rods. There is also the technique of *Spey* casting (similar to the roll), which is performed with a bigger two-handed rod, in rivers where the angler is after salmon or sea trout. It is named after the river where it was first practised; although, in the USA, it is named after another river there: the *Skagit*. Plainly, as Izaak Walton observed in *The Compleat Angler*, a book is nowhere to learn the art and science of angling, any more than it is a place to learn fencing and lessons are necessary. Lessons may be had from, for example, the Hardy Fly Fishing School.

Accessories

A landing net and a creel are the main accessories that you will need. A creel is a wicker basket with a fastening lid and a slot in the top. You line it with moss and dip it in the water where it will keep the catch fresh. As you catch fish you dispatch them with a short cosh, called a 'priest', and place them into the basket through the slot. Other things such as flasks and suggested 'winter warmers' I have already covered under the topic of guns and shooting on pages 34. Besides all that, you will need a holdall bag for all the other equipment, such as food hamper, flies, hooks, spare line, knives for cutting lines, gutting, and so on. If you are going to be fishing in the sun or rain, a parasol or an umbrella is useful as are waterproof coverings and, of course, waders. Farlow's is especially good for all the general gear. Do not forget too that if you are in the hot sun, you should wear a hat and, think about sun-block too.

Seasons

Fishing: Fishing seasons in the UK are (for exact dates, depending on the river): for salmon between January and November; for brown trout between March and October; for sea trout also between March and October. Before undertaking this pursuit, you should acquaint yourself with the current law, including licences, for the place in question.

River fishing licensing and fees.

Any angler aged twelve or over, fishing for salmon, trout, freshwater fish or eels in England (except in the River Tweed, which is separately regulated), Wales, or the Border Esk and its tributaries in Scotland must have a valid Environment Agency rod licence; of which there are two types and the more expensive includes a licence to fish for salmon and migratory trout. There are full season licences, as well as eight and one day licences and concessionary rates for the under sixteens and over sixty fives. It is an offence, punishable by fine, to angle without a relevant licence.

River fishing etiquette

Generally, keep your distance of other anglers; gradually move downstream; don't cross other anglers' water (go around them by the bank); down your rod and offer to lend a hand if you see someone land a big fish; don't wade past the midstream and don't cast towards your own bank; return coloured salmon (that are spawning) and remember not to take kelts (salmon, herling or sea trout which have spawned) and are returning, exhausted, to the ocean. Acquaint yourself with, and obey, the law and respect private property rights. Be generally friendly and helpful to other anglers but remember that some people just want to be left alone. Don't light fires (although you might use a small stove), or leave rubbish (including pieces of line) lying around and try to leave the location as you found it.

Deep sea game fishing

Blue Marlin (*Makaira nigricans*) is one of the most favoured quarry, redolent of Ernest Hemingway's story *The Old Man And The Sea*.

As it happens, down this way, off the coast of Canavieiras (between Salvador and Vitoria in Brazil), are caught the world's biggest Blue Marlin (at up to around five hundred pounds in weight) and in some of the best conditions for fishing for them. The fishing grounds are sited thirteen nautical miles offshore and run for some fifty-eight nautical miles. Besides these fish, there is fishing also for wahoo (*Acanthocybium solandri*), dorado (*Coryphaena hippurus*), tuna (genus *Thunnus*), amberjack (genus *Seriola*), sailfish (*Istiophorus albicans*) and white marlin (*Tetrapturus albidus*). September to December is the best time here, to catch migrating fish. One company that offers very good deals for those seeking the ultimate fishing experience is fishingbluemarlin.com.

Generally speaking, unless you have your own boat and crew and devote yourself to the sport of deep sea game fishing as a way of life, the packages available for this kind of fishing are all-in in terms of equipment and supervision and it would, in a book of this size, be fanciful to go into the suppliers of equipment.

CHAPTER 3

Country Sports – Falconry

I would be a falcon and go free.
I tread her wrist and wear the hood,
Talking to myself, and would draw blood.

From *My Mother Would Be A Falconress,* by Robert Duncan

A Glossary of terms

This is a sport in which there are many special terms, including:

Anklets – are to attach the jesses to the bird's legs.
Austringer – one who trains and flies goshawks.
Aylmeri – a modern fitting for jesses.
Bate – a hawk's jumping to fly while tethered.
Bewet – ties to attach the bells (bells are the traditional method of tracking birds).
Block – a falcon's perch.
Blood – new feather growth.
Bow – a hawk's perch.
Braces – are attached to the hood to close or open it.
Brancher – a young hawk emerging from the nest.
Broad-wing – a bird in the genus *Buteo* or *Parabuteo*.
Cadge – a frame for carrying a number of falcons at once.
Carrying – a bird trying to escape with its kill.
Cast – this has several meanings:

(1) A regurgitated pellet;
(2) A flight of two falcons together;
(3) Launching the bird from the fist, and
(4) Holding a hawk or falcon in order to put on bells and anklets.

Chaps – leggings to protect bird's legs against squirrels' teeth.

Cope – is to file a beak or talons to sharpen them.

Creance – a training line, often fifty yards long.

Dummy bunny – a dummy for training broad-wings.

Enter – a hawk or falcon's first kill.

Eyass – a young bird on the nest.

Falcon – strictly this is the female peregrine falcon but refers to any of the genus *Falco*.

Follow on – a bird following its trainer through the trees in pursuit of quarry.

Foot – the bird grasping the falconer with its talons.

Gauntlet – falconer's glove (traditionally on the left hand).

Giant hood – box in which birds travel.

Hack – to prepare a bird for release to the wild state, sometimes including re-trapping it for flying at quarry.

Haggard – an adult wild bird at least two years old.

Halsband – also called a *jangoli*, this is a strap to propel the bird and is not used in the West, being traditionally Turkish.

Hard-penned – when fully feathered or moulted.

Hawk box – also called a *giant hood* is a travelling box.

Hood – the cap over a bird's head to keep it calm.

Imp – to repair a feather using a previosly moulted one from the same location on wing or tail

Imprint – a bird that recognises itself as human (hand reared).

Intermewed – a bird kept through its moult.

Jack – strictly, the male merlin.

Jesses – the leg straps to hold a hawk.

Leash – a leather to tie the hawk to the fist or perch.

Long-wing – A bird of the genus *Falco*.

Lure – for hawks or falcons, to train them to return.

Make-in – to approach the bird with its prey.

Mangalah – also called a *mankalah* a sturdy cuff-covering used instead of a gauntlet (Arabian only).

Manning – taming a hawk.

Mantle – the bird spreading its wings and covering its prey.

Mews – housing for raptors.

Mute – falcon's droppings.

Passage – an immature wild hawk caught on migration.

Pitch –the height at which a hawk hovers.

Put over – moving food from crop to stomach.

Quarry – prey.

Ring perch – on which a hawk might sit.

Rouse – hawk shaking its feathers.

Short-wing – a hawk of the genus *Accipter*.

Slice – bird propelling droppings away from the perch or nest.

Stoop – the bent-winged dive towards the quarry.

Swivel – a device to prevent tangles in the jesses and the leash.

Tail guard – to protect tail feathers.

Talon – claw.

Telemetry – a system for bird tracking by means of transmitter and receiver.

Tercel – strictly, a male peregrine falcon.

Wait-on – a falcon circling and awaiting the flush.

Yagi – aerial in telemetry system of tracking.

Yarak – a goshawk in good hunting condition.

History

Falconry is defined by statute as follows: '*Falconry is the pursuit of wild quarry in its natural state by means of trained birds of prey.*' It has been known from ancient times, especially in the Middle and Far East and there are various schools: the European school uses falcons and hawks; the Mid-Asian school uses eagles (even hunting wolves with them) and hawks; the Middle Eastern school, which uses falcons, and the Oriental school, which uses hawks and falcons.

Interestingly, hunted prey is halal for Muslims but it is not kosher for Jews. The sport was possibly introduced into Britain in the ninth century AD where it remained a favourite country sport for hundreds of years, until the development of reasonably accurate shot guns. It was also seen as a status symbol to the extent that there were even laws of ownership imposed to control the birds that one could fly, according to one's social rank. The Normans even went so far as to provide that all hawks belonged to the Crown. However, by the reign of Henry III, freemen could own hawks. Statute of Henry VII gave hawks full protection.

The birds could (and can) be trained to catch aerial or ground prey. Hooding the birds, prior to release, is one way that has always been employed to keep the birds calm until the 'off'.

There are three main categories of birds: short, broad and long-winged. Short-winged birds are the hawks. Broad-winged birds are eagles and buzzards. Long-winged birds are falcons and peregrines and peregrines are not just the fastest birds but the fastest animals on earth; well out-stripping the cheetah and the swallow, and reaching nearly two hundred miles an hour in the stoop.

Raptors are magnificent and costly birds but falconry is not for the faint-hearted; it is necessary to understand that a raptor is 'not just for Christmas' and that it will need a lot of attention and care every day. Moreover, with injured prey, you need to be able and willing to dispatch it forthwith, to avoid unnecessary suffering.

The British Hawk Board represents UK falconry through national and local clubs and there are many schools and falconry centres too.

The best thing to do before you launch into this sport and buy a bird, is to join a local club (there are around twenty-three in the UK) and to get under the wing of an experienced falconer or austringer. Get to handle the birds and watch them being slipped and in action. Get yourself on a course, where you can learn from the outset, the basics of bird handling and control. There are thirty-five training centres in the UK. Always bear in mind that you need, as well as any necessary game licence, the landowner's permission to hunt over his land; only fly one bird at a time and set it only on prey that you are happy that it can kill and, of course, that is not itself protected by legislation. Have regard for other users of the land, especially children, as well as the well-being of your bird and, especially, watch out for the presence of hazards, such as dogs, power lines and people who are shooting.

Nowadays, there is also a big market for falconry in relation to pest control in city centres; at airports and landfill sites.

The Types of Birds Often Used

The Peregrine Falcon (*Falco peregrinus*), the Goshawk (*Accipter gentilis*), Golden Eagle (*Aquila chrysaetos*) and the Sparrow hawk (*Accipter nisus*) are the main hawks encountered in the sport in the Old World. Of Buzzards, the Red-tailed hawk (*Buteo jamaicensis*) and Harris Hawk (*Parabuteo unicinctus*) are the most commonly used in the USA and Europe and, of the Falcons, there is the Barbary falcon (*Falco peregrinus pelegrinoides*); Gyrfalcon (*Falco rusticolus*); Peregrine falcon (*Falco peregrinus*), and the little Merlin (*Falco columbarius*), which used to be the usual ladies' falcon. Flying Aplomado Falcons (*Falco femoralis*) becomes more popular in the New World. Hawks are sprinters and tend to go for ground prey or take birds as they flush and the falcons go for aerial prey taking birds in flight. How you choose the type of bird is very much a personal decision; sensibly influenced by the landscape, available quarry and environment in which you will hunt.

Regulation

The keeping of raptors is highly regulated in the UK (and also elsewhere) and they fall within Schedule 4 to the Wildlife and Countryside Act 1981 and need to be registered and ringed, according to legislation administered by DEFRA. The onus is on the keeper to demonstrate that the birds in his possession are lawfully there and not taken from the wild (except for so long as they may be kept while injured). Bear this carefully in mind when you are buying a bird, as there are criminal penalties for infringing the law. It has, in the past, been possible to get a licence to take a raptor from the wild but no such licences have been granted for a long time. This is probably because there is such a healthy number bred in captivity: it is estimated that there are twenty-five thousand in the UK alone; with two thousand breeders and five thousand active falconers. Some owners do not necessarily take part in falconry as such but just take pleasure in keeping these graceful creatures. Moreover, depending where you are in the UK, you might need a game licence for flying them and you are also obliged to have regard to the game seasons.

Housing

There are two principal concerns: first size and security and, secondly, cleanliness. The Hawk Board recommends that accommodation should be at least twice the bird's wingspan in length and breadth but, plainly, the bigger the accommodation, the happier your bird will be. Make sure that it is soundly protected against vermin and other creatures that could harm your bird and clean the quarters regularly, as these birds are susceptible to a range of diseases and complaints as well as nervousness if they are not handled properly. Just out of interest, the word 'mews' now referring to the housing in small lanes behind larger houses in London and other cities, derives from the fact that falcons used to be housed in these buildings, demonstrating just how popular the sport was.

Equipment

The equipment that you will need will include: a falconry vest, food pouches (to reward the bird), gauntlet, hoods for the bird, swivels (to avoid tangling the jesses) and a good book on the subject, such as that by Dr Nick Fox, mentioned in the Bibliography. You will also need a hawk box which should be well-ventilated but dark and secure and big enough to allow the bird to stand upright inside. It is as well to have a first aid pack to hand as accidents can happen and having, as a minimum, a vial of iodine and plasters is certainly a good idea.

Feeding and watering

Make sure that your bird has a constant supply of clean water and an appropriate diet to enable it to maintain maximum fitness: this means that the bird should be lean and well-muscled and certainly not fat. They need meat in whole bird and small mammal form and raw meat. Advice on diet and amounts of food is available in the book, mentioned above and there is a farm called Honeybrook Farm which provides food for raptors and reptiles.

Useful Organizations

In relation to a wealth of information, including that relating to courses and training, there are: the British Falconers' Club and falconryforum.co.uk and similar organizations in other countries. The Falconry Heritage Trust exists to record the history of falconry and to promote the sport. A very useful overview of falconry as it is currently practised is given in the Audit, by Nick Fox and Jim Chick, mentioned in the Bibliography; from which the statistics, cited above, derive. In 2010 UNESCO recognized falconry in fourteen countries as an activity of 'intangible cultural heritage' and this affords protection, whilst allowing the sport to develop for future generations to enjoy.

CHAPTER 4

Country Sports – Hunting, Steeple Chases, Hacking

The dusky night rides down the sky,
And ushers in the morn;
The hounds all join in glorious cry,
The huntsman winds his horn:
And a-hunting we will go.

Henry Fielding

Introduction

Man has hunted with hounds (practised *venery*) since time immemorial and prehistoric man began the domestication of wild dogs and wolves for the purpose. The ancient Sumerians in Mesopotamia had dogs and they travelled far and wide for trade and took their dogs all over the known world. Besides hunting, dogs were also anciently used in war (hence the expression 'dogs of war'). The ancient Egyptians and other North Africans had their Molossian dogs, the Chinese, long ago, had their Pekinese and the Celts, the Romans and the Greeks all hunted with hounds.

Gradually there developed, over centuries, different types of sporting hounds and dogs: sight hounds; scent hounds; pointers and retrievers. English and American foxhounds are scent hounds. Besides the foxhounds, there are also the smaller beagles and harriers, which are used for hare hunting.

Despite attempted abolition in several places, hunting with hounds survives. The sportsmen and the supporters say that it is continuing within the law and the law enforcement authorities, thankfully, seem to lack much enthusiasm for investigating the subject.

As in so many country sporting activities, strict observance of the requirements of safety and displaying a faultless courtesy (even to the '*antis*'), will take you far; no matter how many times you are thrown from your horse (or how many birds glide, low and contemptuous, over your head).

Ride a quiet horse that is easy to stop and that takes its fences (there is a specific type called a 'hunter'). Make sure that it is well groomed, trimmed and neatly tacked, without ornament; although your horse should be plaited for the opening meet and lawn meets. Keep your distance of others and bring your horse to face the hounds and not back-end on; if it kicks, it should wear a red ribbon on its tail. Don't wear colognes out hunting (as this could disturb the scent that the hounds are after); or any chains etc., that could get caught in branches. In wet weather members may be allowed by the Master to wear riding macs strapped to the legs; either over, or in place of, hunt coats. When you arrive at the meet, be on time and greet the Master and advise the field secretary of your presence. Always salute the landowner if you see him or her. Ride behind, and give way to, members who have their colours (the right, awarded by the Master, to wear the coloured hunt coat and hunt buttons), which are earned over time by displaying good horsemanship, a regard for the well-being of the hunt and its members; the general promotion of the hunt, and a concern for safety and courtesy. Never, ever, overtake the Master and generally keep behind all full members of the hunt with their colours and the staff. If your horse refuses a jump, go (out of safety and courtesy) to the back of the line. If you need to withdraw, tell the Master or the secretary and leave, if possible by metalled roads. If you are 'excused' the hunt by the Master, for some misdemeanour, you go home in disgrace.

Glossary of terms not otherwise explained

Antis – hunt abolitionists.
Babbling – hounds unnecessarily in cry, giving voice.
Biddable – responsive (of hounds).
Break-up – the eating of the fox by the hounds.
Cap/Field money – a sum paid to the hunt treasurer or secretary for the day's hunting.
Casting hounds – spreading them out.
'Charlie' – Mr Fox (sometimes also 'Mr Todd').
Check – lose the scent of the quarry.
Couple – hounds are counted in 'couples'.
Draw – draw hounds through the coverts.
Field – hunt followers, except 'antis'.
Field money – see 'Cap money' above.
Foiled – of scent – lost scent.
Gate please! – instruction to open the gate.
Gone to earth/ground – self-explanatory.
Headland please! – instruction to cross by the unploughed part of a field.

Hold hard! – stop and wait.

Huntsman please! – instruction to make way for the huntsman.

Lawn meets – meets on the lawns of private houses and estates.

Opening meet – first meet of the season.

Pads – dead fox's feet.

Point – distance from the putting-up to the point where the quarry is broken up or lost.

Riot of hounds – hounds out of control and chasing a cat or dog or other creature.

Rolled-over – killed.

Subscription – annual amount for hunt membership for individuals or families.

'Tally-ho! Away' – cry when quarry is put-up.

'Tally-ho! Back' – cry when quarry returns to the coverts.

'Tally-ho! Across' – cry when quarry crosses a road etc.

Hunt Clothing

Besides the general description of hunt clothing in my book *History of Men's Fashion*, a few more words are appropriate here, as well as the observation that there are slight variations in specificity of detail from hunt to hunt and it is best to seek clarification on any point of doubt from the hunt secretary.

For autumnal cub-hunting, the informal tweed hacking jacket and accoutrements are appropriate (the 'rat-catcher' outfit). This makes no distinction between members with colours and those without or, indeed, the hunt staff. The hacking jacket should be predominantly a brown or green, or in other muted colours and, maybe, come in a discreet check or other pattern. The hacking jacket is cut longer than an ordinary sports' coat, has decidedly slanted pockets (for easier access), three buttons down the front (all to be done up while mounted) and a central back vent. It is an idea to have the back of this jacket (or any riding coat for that matter) lined in water and stain resistant material because the back of the jacket is going to spread out over the saddle and the horse's sweaty back (*'horses sweat; gentlemen perspire and ladies merely glow'*). A hunting stock may be worn, as long as it is a coloured stock and not the *formal* hunting white or cream stock. A great supplier of these coloured stocks is silkroutescotland.com .Then there are also Swaine Adeney Brigg and W & H Gidden for riding and hunting clothes and accessories. One word about stocks: they are bound around the neck and become collar and tie in one; properly tied, their bulk and firmness add support to the neck both when riding and in the event of a fall and so their retention as part of hunting dress is not just a retrocentric yearning for *les neiges d'antan*. As always for hunt members, the plain stock pin (three inches long, in gold, for gentlemen), should be positioned horizontally (athwart) and through the folds. If necessary, ask someone to demonstrate to you how to tie a hunting stock properly (with the final crossed-over folds) and do not take the short cut of simply tying it like an informal cravat. Otherwise a pale, plain or lightly patterned shirt and suitable, darker tie is fine.

Besides those mentioned in the first edition of my book *History of Men's Fashion*, I just mention another few excellent (but less generally known), shirtmakers (whether for hunting or ordinary day shirts): Frank Foster is the first and he has made shirts for a host of Hollywood stars, such as Ray Milland; Cary Grant; Sean Connery; Topol; not to mention Dizzy Gillespie and he even made Peter O'Toole's robes for the film *Lawrence of Arabia*. He is based in Pall Mall. The second other shirtmaker that must be mentioned is Sean O'Flynn, who also enjoys a high reputation; he works out of Meyer & Mortimer in Sackville Street. The third is Stephen Lachter, now with tailors John Kent and Terry Haste in New Burlington Street. Watch out for the signed picture of Frank Sinatra on the wall: 'For Stephen – You make a great shirt! My very best to you – Frank Sinatra. 1980.'

Breeches for the informal hunting rig should be beige, buff, rust or canary but not any dark colour. These will probably be made of cloth, such as cavalry twill, but proper breeches should really be made of buckskin and incorporate instead of the modern fly, full or split 'falls' – basically a buttoned flap (with two rows of buttons for full falls and one row for split falls) and, of course, brace buttons for your box cloth Thurston braces.

Real buckskin is made from the buffed-up grain-side of the skin of deer or elk and 'nubuck' is made from the buffed-up grain-side of calf (distinguished from suede, which is made from the flesh-side of (usually) calf). The flesh-side of deerskin (the suede side), is called *split* deerskin. Often 'nubuck' is substituted for real buckskin.

Brown field boots are normal (but not of the lacing variety). Schnieder Boots (with W & H Gidden in Clifford Street), supply great ready to wear boots.

A gentleman's velvet hunt cap in black or a black extra firm hunting bowler (or 'coke') hat are usually worn. There is also a square crowned variety, called a 'Cambridge' (seldom used for riding) but these now have to be bespoken from Patey Hats. The dress code for certain hunts dictates that dark grey velvet caps are *de rigueur*. The hunt cap's ribbons should always, for members of the hunt (with certain exceptions), be tucked inside, sewn or tied up. There was a time when just the Master, the hunt servants and farmers wore the hunt cap but this is no longer so. If the bowler (or coke) hat is chosen it should also have attached to it a black hat cord.

I would suggest that for all 'hard' hats such as bowlers, top hats and velvet hunt caps the *conformateur* (as described in *History of Men's Fashion*) is used to take the shape of the head and that each and every hat is therefore shaped to fit the individual's head-shape and when properly fitted a hunt cap will stay put on the head – over hill, ditch and hedge. When correctly fitted, the Patey velvet hunt cap is sometimes fondly referred to as having a 'suction fit', so snuggly but comfortably does it adhere to the contours of the rider's head. A cord is a prudent addition to a bowler or top hat – the cord tends to be for those who are riding in very rough terrain which is less often the case nowadays because, over the years, hedges and field boundaries have been removed in many rural areas. Patey's riding headwear the top hat, bowler and the velvet hunt cap (best worn without a harness as this is more elegant and the purist way), are the most traditional of riding hats, using techniques which have been handed down over the generations, from Huguenot forebears, who brought to London the hat-making skills they used to produce exquisite hats for the Paris élite of the eighteenth century. These skills form the basis of the 'hard' hats' techniques used at Patey's today.

Hard hats are completely made from scratch – starting with the making of the raw materials from which the hard base of the hat is made – using a type of linen known as mull or gossamer, which is coated with coodle, a shellac-based paste. Shellac is a varnish-like substance derived from an Indian beetle (*Laccifer lacca*), which is, incidentally also the material from which vintage records were made and someone involved in the promotion of shellac told Janet Taylor of Patey's, that it is even used to give a fine sheen to certain manufactured chocolates and sweets!

Shellac on riding hats is built up in layers to form a solid sheet of 'goss' . This is left to cure for five months and then it is cut into strips and built up by hand on a block to form the shell or hard base of a top hat, bowler or hunt cap. This takes an additional five hours' work, the hard hat base is left to dry for a week and then the block removed. All of this takes place before the final hat is covered, trimmed and lined.

For formal hunting, a white or cream stock is *de rigueur* and vests are usually either canary yellow or incorporate a light Tattersall checked pattern. If you are without your hunt's colours, you will wear a black hunting jacket and plain buttons; buff breeches and black boot garters with butcher boots or a plain black frock coat (again with plain buttons); white breeches and white boot garters with butcher boots. If you have your hunt's colours, you will be similarly attired, except that your black buttons will bear the hunt's badge etched in white and you should wear boots with tops; although black butcher boots are acceptable with the shorter hunt jacket. The lighter tops on top boots derive from the fact that riding boots used to be worn over the knee and, on entering a house, wearers used to fold the tops down to hide the mud and so expose the lighter boot linings.

Scarlet or coats in the hunt's colours (if different) are optional for members with colours. These have gold buttons bearing the hunt's badge; are single-vented (as are all riding coats) and have three buttons and, even with frocks for most members with colours, rounded front skirts. Coloured coats are especially appropriate (for those entitled to wear them) for the opening meet, the blessing of the hounds and New Year's Day, as well as when hosting a joint meet. These coats and jackets are usually made of Melton cloth.

Some say that the phrase '*in the pink*', denoting happiness, or superlative state, derives from the satisfaction which customers felt in wearing hunting coats which a tailor, supposedly called Thomas Pink, made in the eighteenth century; although there is a reference, long before, in Shakespeare's Romeo and Juliet, Act 2, Scene IV, line 57, dated 1597, to being '*in the pink*':Mercutio: '*Nay, I am in the very pink of courtesy.*' and there is not any known documentary evidence to support the assertion that there even was any such tailor as Thomas Pink at all: possibly, another urban legend.

There are alternatives to the velvet hunt cap, with the formal hunting attire. An extra firm hunting (old silk or new felt) top hat is appropriate for a coloured coat or a black frock. An extra firm hunting bowler (or coke) is appropriate with a black hunting jacket. The hat cord is black, although it used to be red with a red coat or jacket.

Janet Taylor, formerly of James Lock & Co and now of Patey Hats, established in 1799 (the only British gentleman's bespoke hat maker left, with a new shop in Connaught Street, London W2), says that the top hat (as we might recognize the modern item), was invented by a Frenchman and it probably does originally derive from a Continental design. Prior to being called top hats, they were merely called silk hats or beaver hats. Before silk was used, most were made of lustrous beaver fur felt. References to 'beaver hats' go back long before the hats that we would recognize as a modern top hat (such as cocked hats), and so it is difficult to pinpoint the exact moment of creation of the forerunner of the modern top hat. Moreover, so far as the shape of the top hat is concerned, there are representations of tall, cylindrical hats that go back into ancient history and there are even references to beaver hats in humorous verse:

> On the top of the Crumpetty Tree
> The Quangle Wangle sat,
> But his face you could not see,
> On account of his Beaver Hat.

For his hat was a hundred and two feet wide,
With ribbons and bibbons on every side
And bells, and buttons, and loops, and lace,
So that nobody ever could see the face
Of the Quangle Wangle Quee.

Edward Lear

As I mention in *History of Men's Fashion*, there is the popular urban legend that a clothier, called John Hetherington, was the first man to wear a silk top hat in the streets of London, in early 1797, when it caused a riot and he was bound over to keep the peace. Some versions of the story even go so far as to name him as the actual inventor of the silk top hat, or top hats in general.

However, this should now be read in connection with the discovery of references (in the West Sussex Records Office), to (George) Dunnage & (Thomas) Larkin, described in a bill, dated 1798, to the then Lord Egremont, as makers of 'waterproof silk hats' and the Guildhall Library has records of insurance, dated 1806, by the Sun Fire Insurance Co, over that firm's property at 424 Strand, when they were described as 'silk hat manufacturers'. There are other records in the National Archives, dated 1807 -1818, in which several firms are described as manufacturers of silk hats. A little later still there are references to 'stovepipe hats'.

Ascot Top Hats Ltd have gathered evidence that Dunnage first made a form of hat, using a silk shag (hatters plush) as 'imitation of beaver' in 1793. The invention was approved as a patent (2022 of 1794) and the firm of Dunnage & Larkin continued to be patent silk hat manufactures until dissolution of their silk hat business in 1814. This evidence is supplemented by a book of the Dunnage family history, written by George Dunnage's descendant, Louise Buckingham (listed in the bibliography) and by a further patent (2273 of 1798), for a ventilating *top* hat (as we would recognize it), made of waterproof silk (for coachmen).

This all means that it is reasonably possible that it was George Dunnage & Thomas Larkin who created the first silk top hats in Britain; although the hatter Lincoln Bennett was also an early pioneer of silk in imitation of beaver in hat-making and was another early maker of top hats.

I would suggest that it would have been necessary for a form of silk plush to have been available prior to the Hetherington story (from 1797). It was developed as a substitute for beaver felt, which was in short supply. Silk would then have been used on all styles of hats, including tricorn and bicorn cocked hats, probably used over a rigid goss base; a method still used by Patey's when making the Lord Mayor of London's tricorn hat.

With any style of hat it is extremely difficult to pin-point the very first of a type. I would suggest that the Hetherington story has been handed down and become the focus of the birth of the silk top hat but (if it is not just a legend), it could well have been not the very first but one of the first of its type.

Hunting weight top hats are hand made on extra firm weight shells and now covered in felt and treated at Patey's with a special finish, which weatherproofs them but do *not* use boot polish or Guinness. Patey's treat all hunting weight toppers in their workroom with waterproofing, added with hot irons; this is, in fact, the most traditional of procedures and they do not supply this proofing to customers because the skill of applying it is best not tried at home!

Maybe, this arcane secret is redolent of Beau Brummell who, when asked how he made his famously shiny black, leather boots gleam, to paraphrase, replied 'only the finest of champagne…'

Any of the current hatters mentioned above could supply suitable hunting hats (together with the other second hand sources, which I mention in *History of Men's Fashion*) but only Patey's still hand-make them in the UK and they offer a bespoke service too. They also supply reconditioned silk top hats, for Ascot and so forth, honed to perfection, with the black glossy gleam of a vintage record.

Wearing formal hats and something more of soft felts

All formal hats – for example, toppers, cokes and hunt caps – are properly worn to sit more or less straight on the head but, in the case of toppers and cokes, tilted slightly forward – but not at a rakish angle, which might be appropriate to soft felts, panamas and tweed hats and caps. On the subject of soft felt hats: the trilby hat is named after George du Maurier's late nineteenth century novel and play, *Trilby*; because one of the protagonists, Little Billee, is 'discovered' wearing such a hat. The heroine, Trilby O'Ferrall, an artist's foot model, was mesmerized by the evil, controlling Svengali. George Palmella Busson du Maurier (1834–1896) enjoyed a youthful career as a Bohemian artist in Paris, before he settled in Hampstead, North London. He worked as a cartoonist for *Punch* and his most famous cartoon was *True Humility* (1895), from which we get the familiar expression 'a Curate's egg'; the cartoon is reproduced in Plate 16 and the caption ran:

Bishop: 'I'm afraid you've got a bad egg, Mr Jones'
Curate: 'Oh, no, My Lord. I assure you! Parts of it are excellent.'

George was the grandfather of the even more successful novelist, Daphne du Maurier.

The higher-crowned, broader-brimmed fedora hat is also named after a fictional character: the heroine of Victorien Sardou's 1882 play, *Fédora*.

Besides all this gear (for both the informal and formal hunting), you will need a horn-handled, hunting whip (with a silver button in the horn and lash in the colour appropriate to your hunt), a pocket or a 'bayonet' saddle hunting flask, a sandwich box, your snuff box and a decent handkerchief or two. For excellent vintage whips and flasks, try sportingcollection.com. and also fieldand countryantiques.co.uk. The curved horn handle of the traditional hunting whip is useful for opening and closing latches on any gates that you do not jump! – although hunts, often have members appointed to close gates. The lash can be shaken at hounds to keep them away for your horse's feet.

Conspicuous jewellery and (subject to below), buttonholes, are not appropriate for hunting. Keep the jewellery down to the stockpin and a watch; closed-face 'hunter' fob watches were originally designed to protect the glass and face of the watch in any fall from the horse. Hunting shirts normally have either button cuffs or stretchable fitted cuffs, so cufflinks are not necessary and could even cause injury in a fall.

Some hold that violets used to be worn as hunting buttonholes, on certain occasions before the Second World War; maybe this practice derived from the myth of Attis (beloved of the mother goddess Cybele), who was killed while hunting a boar, when his blood, spilled on the ground, brought forth violets.

There are internet sites run by the Master of Foxhounds Associations for England and Wales (mfha.org.uk); Ireland (imfha.com) and America (mfha.org) and these are useful in locating hunts and organizers; even if some of their organizers are not (as I have found), tremendously dynamic in pursuing means of advertising the merits of hunting. There are also fox hunts in Australia, Canada, France, India, Italy and Russia.

Harrier packs and Boar Hunting in France

There are still also harrier and beagle packs in existence, where the field is on foot. Harriers and beagles hunt hares. There are also three remaining stag hunts (in the West Country).

There is a photograph that I have seen of Winston Churchill (nearly as fond as George IV of uniforms and dress generally), boar hunting near Dieppe in France, in 1928, with his son Randolph and Coco Chanel, in which he is wearing a fur-lined, long black overcoat and a hunt cap. Of course, after the Second World War (when she holed-up with a Nazi officer in the Paris Ritz), Coco went out of favour with such as Churchill and the post-war British Ambassador in Paris, Duff (with Diana) Cooper. Boar hunting in France and parts of Europe also continues.

Hunt Balls and something of a remarkable character

Hunt balls are still held and the degree of formality varies from hunt to hunt. They used to be affairs at which full evening dress was worn and full gentlemen-members of the hunt would wear scarlet (or other appropriate hunt-coloured) dress coats and black breeches or evening trousers. Other colours include Oxford blue (with ivory *revers*) for the exclusive Oxford undergraduate Bullingdon Club, which was founded around 1780, as a hunting and cricket club but nowadays concentrates on dining and raising Cain. The colours of the Beaufort Hunt (one of the oldest, dating back, in some form, to 1682) are blue with ivory *revers*. The Quorn claims to be the oldest regularly organized *fox* hunt, dating back to 1696.

Nowadays, often dinner jackets and black tie are permitted but scarlet swallow-tail evening coats are still seen; although seldom with such details as cut-on lapels, formed cuffs, recessed silk *revers* and buttons on the bottom of the back skirts. The modern prescription of full evening dress for a hunt ball is: a scarlet (or other hunt colour) barathea dress coat (lined in matching silk), with silk *revers* in the colour appropriate to the hunt, with gilt buttons bearing the badge of the hunt; otherwise as a standard dress coat (including pockets inside the tails); over a stiff-fronted, white, marcella shirt with a detachable, stiff wing collar and white marcella tie. The waistcoat is also white Marcella; in this case, with *four* buttons and long points.

The waistcoat buttons might be miniature gilt hunt buttons or, for any *roués* still at large, diamond-set gilt buttons. Diamonds would be redolent of the Regency, Antiguan plantation owner and amateur actor, Robert Coates (1772–1848), whose nicknames ranged between 'Curricle', 'Diamond' and 'Romeo' Coates. The nickname 'Curricle' derived from his habit of driving around town in an ornamented curricle, which was a chariot drawn by a fine pair of white horses, harnessed abreast, at the canter. The word curricle derives from the Latin *curriculum* (track for chariot racing) and the Latin *currere* (to run).

According to contemporary accounts, this curricle was one of the neatest vehicles in London. Its carriage work was fashioned in the shape of a scallop shell, painted in a rich lake blue, bearing painted representations of Coates's crest, a cock with outspread wings, under the motto '*While I live, I'll crow.*' The step, a bar decoration and parts of the harnesses were also in the form of a cock. This led to him acquiring yet another *soubriquet*: 'Cock-a-doodle-doo' Coates. There were two high wheels and light springs and inside it was well and richly upholstered. It came to be well known around Long Acre, the parishes of St James's and St George's, the Row and even in the City, where it was sometimes parked outside the Bank of England, while its rich owner was attending to his investments inside.

The nickname 'Diamond' derived from his big, diamond adornments, including diamond buttons, diamond knee and shoe buckles and a diamond hat decoration, and the nickname 'Romeo' derived from his ludicrous attempts to play that part in Shakespeare's play *Romeo and Juliet*, in which even his costume did nothing to delight the groundlings, or even the bucks and beaux in the audience. A contemporary account mentions a spangled cloak of sky blue, crimson pantaloons and a plumed white hat (as well as all the diamonds already mentioned). At his *début*, in the part, at Bath (on 9 February 1810), the audience reaction included cries of 'Off! Off! Off!' But, to this, apart from expressing his own scorn (by folding his arms and staring at his detractors), he seems to have been, then and always, stubbornly indifferent. According to one observer of a later performance: *'On this occasion no life was lost, as nothing harder than orange peel was thrown...'*

Poor old Coates (also known as *'The Celebrated Amateur of Fashion'*), after having squandered most of his fortune, according to one wry commentator, died after having been run over by an *'inferior'* coach. In fact he attended a concert at Drury Lane on 15 February 1848 and, afterwards, having got into his carriage, he remembered that he had left his treasured opera glasses in the box and, re-crossing Russell Street to fetch them, he seems to have been knocked down by a *'carelessly and furiously driven'* hansom cab. Despite the fact that the inquest jury returned a verdict of manslaughter (by a person unknown), no one was ever brought to book for the incident and Coates died of complications from his injuries in his house at 28 Montagu Square, London W1, on 21 February.

It would be wrong to leave the subject of Robert Coates, which I have treated with some levity, without mentioning that many of the theatrical performances for which Coates had been so savagely criticized and reviled, he had in fact put on to raise money for charitable causes (he had liked to be known as *'The Celebrated Philanthropic Amateur'*) and, although he had many critics, he also had his admirers. Maybe, they most admired his courage and his persistence but it must also be said that the monologues, which he sometimes delivered after the drama was over, sometimes met with general, enthusiastic appreciation. Moreover, although Beau Brummell has been suggested by his recent biographer, Ian Kelly, to have been 'the first modern celebrity', this is an unlikely description of a man whose fame, for restraint in dress and manners (whose preference was to be conveyed in the seclusion of a curtained sedan chair), was restricted to (at most), the three thousand or so members of the upper class of his age. Much the same goes for the Count d'Orsay. Coates, on the other hand, was known, through his dramatic performances, to a much wider population and so has a greater claim than either Brummell or D'Orsay; especially since the attainment of 'modern celebrity' does not necessarily involve the display of any particular skill or achievement. Moreover, decked out in his costumes and his diamonds and careening around in his curricle, Robert Coates could easily be said to have been the first modern male exponent of *Bling*.

If you are going to have diamond-set waistcoat buttons, you will abandon then the advice on restraint that is given in *History of Men's Fashion*, and have diamond-set front shirt stud(s) too and what about diamond and ruby, *pavé*-set cufflinks? Black satin evening breeches are appropriate, with four silk-covered buttons and a black buckle at each knee plus a fob pocket on the right side of the waistband. The stockings should be black silk, worn over thin, black lisle stockings and the pumps should be ordinary evening pumps with bows (either pinched or flat). An alternative to breeches is a pair of black full dress evening trousers (with the double stripe of ribbon down each leg). White kid evening gloves, silk scarf, an evening cloak (worn with breeches) or (with trousers), a black evening top coat, with silk *revers* and basket-weave silk buttons; a black silk topper or opera hat and a silver-topped ebony stick would finish it all off nicely. But how many would, in this modern age, dare go the whole hog; especially with the breeches and opera cloak?

The more prosaic dinner jacket options, sometimes permitted, are as described in Chapter 5 of *History of Men's Fashion*.

Fox hunting season

Hunting: The formal foxhunting season is from the beginning of November to the beginning of April. Before undertaking this pursuit, you should acquaint yourself with the current law for the place in question. I do not deal with stag hunting and hare coursing. There are Masters of Foxhounds Associations for England, Wales and Scotland; and others for Ireland and the USA. These give information about the various hunts. At the moment there are one hundred and seventy-six packs of hounds in England and Wales and a further ten in Scotland.

Point-to-point steeple chases

These are amateur steeple-chases (originally races between steepled churches as landmarks), arranged by the hunt for members of the hunt or adjoining hunts (or Point-to-Point Clubs), sometimes including open events, for any amateur riders, but on horses that have been hunted enough to qualify for a certificate of entry. Events take place between the end of November to the following June; there may be half a dozen races in any event and, since 1976, ladies have raced on equal terms with the men. The course is set (normally over a three mile course), over natural ground and incorporates a minimum of eighteen natural and artificial jumps, all marked out with flags.

The British Horseracing Authority ('BHA') regulates these races and the Point-to-Point Authority administers them. The first such organized events are claimed by the Worcestershire Hunt (from 1836) but the Atherstone claims the first regularly organized annual events (from 1870). The regulations include provision banning horses professionally trained within the period beginning with 1 November preceding the meeting and certain professional riders; the courses are approved by an inspector.

Here, plainly, the essential articles for participation are: a safety helmet (this has replaced the more cavalier, devil-may-care cap or felt hat and this will be covered in a silk cap with your colours and there are even body protectors (both satisfying minimum safety requirements). You will need light-coloured breeches and light weight boots or light coloured jodhpurs and jodhpur boots; deerskin or peccary gloves and a short cane or a riding crop (for correcting the horse only; since cutting whips and spurs are not permitted). Apart from that, the upper body should be clad in racing silks or something light and suitable to the weather; even a jumper. You will also be required to wear a medical armband, containing all essential information about you; including the name and address of your doctor; your blood group; any medication that you are receiving; any disabilities and allergies that you have, and so on, for quick reference in the event of injury. Anyone intending to take part in such racing should acquaint themselves with the current regulations, made by the BHA and, preferably, read Michael Williams' book, mentioned in the Bibliography. The official website, where (amongst other things), fixtures are listed, is pointtopoint.co.uk.

Suitable dress for spectators at these events is suggested in Chapter 11 of *History of Men's Fashion*.

Hacking

Here, apart from being neatly presented, comfort may prevail and jumpers (including polo-necked jumpers), darker breeches and brown riding boots or Newmarket boots; jodhpurs and jodhpur boots, together with Schofell or Barbour coats, are likely to be preferred over more formal dress. If you are going on highways in poor light, you ought to have reflectors on the tack, and wear a reflective gilet but it is far better to avoid this situation. Always remember to acknowledge courteous motor vehicle drivers, who slow down for you and give way.

The following magazines provide useful news and information about country sports: *Country Life*; *Horse and Hound*; *The Angling Times*; *The Falconers and Raptor Conservation Magazine*; *The Field*; *The Shooting Times* as well as the website gofishing.co.uk. Also see: *Baily's Hunting Directory*.

Plate 1: A cartoon of a pistol duel, from an original cartoon, by Thomas Rowlandson (1756-1827).

Plate 2: A pair of duelling pistols, by Robert Wogdon, from a private collection. The photograph is by courtesy of the owner.

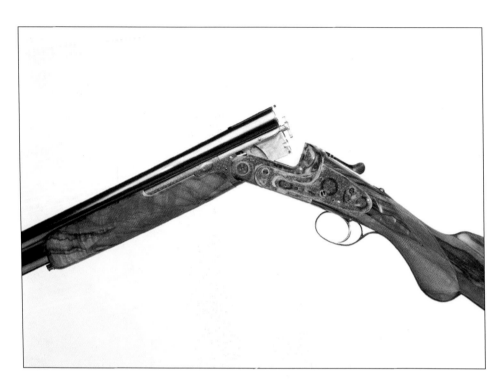

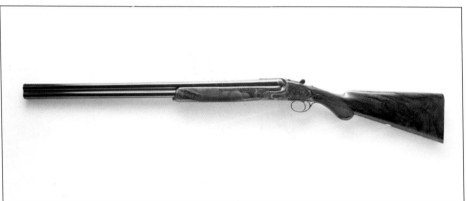

Plates 3–6: London Best shotguns, by Boss & Co. Photographs by courtesy of Boss & Co.

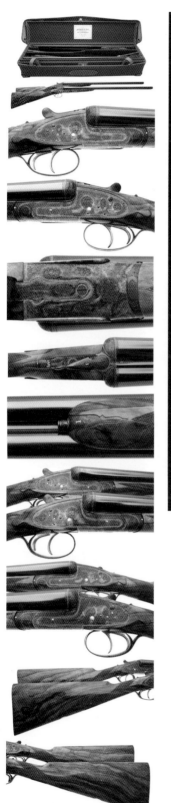
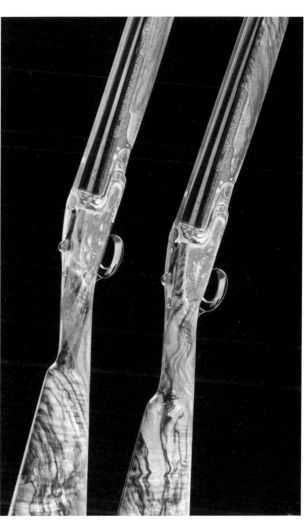

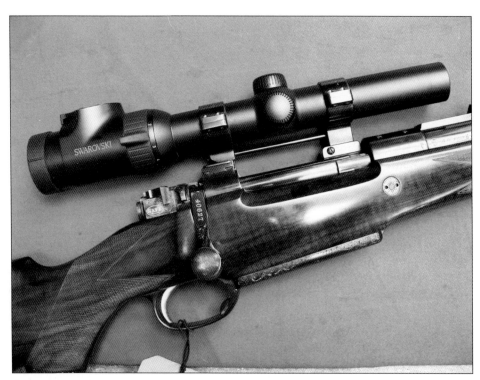

Plate 7:.416 calibre Big Game bolt action sporting rifle, by W J Jeffrey & Co. Photograph by courtesy of J Roberts & Son.

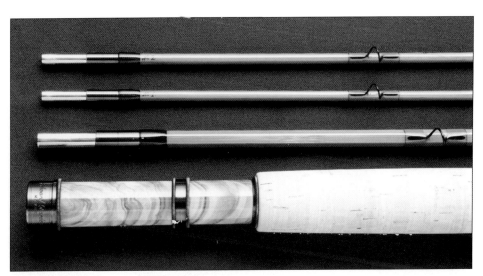

Plate 8–9: Split cane fly fishing rods, by Edward Barder. Photographs by courtesy of Edward Barder.

Plate 10: A Falconer; from an
original drawing by Dr Alfred
E Brehm (1829–1884).

Plate 11: Lord Ribblesdale (1854–1925),
dressed for hunting; from an original portrait,
by John Singer Sargent (1856–1925).

Plate 12–14: A hunting top hat; a hunting bowler hat and a hunt cap, by Patey Hats. Photographs by courtesy of Patey Hats.

Plate 15: Robert 'Curricle' – 'Diamond' – 'Romeo' Coates (1772-1848), from an old engraving.

Plate 16:

Bishop: "I am afraid you've got a bad egg, Mr Jones!"
Curate: "Oh, no, my Lord, I assure you! Parts of it are excellent."

From the original cartoon, *True Humility*, by George du Maurier (1834-1896), first published in *Punch*, on 19th November 1895.

Plate 17: A view of St James's Square, London; facing west towards King Street. Photograph by courtesy of Erin Shipley, Westminster City Archives.

Plate 18: A view of the harbour of Fowey, Cornwall; "The dearest of small cities." Photograph by courtesy of JS Storey.

Plate 19: The Foundation Sire, 'The Darley Arabian', from an original painting, by John Wootton (1682–1764).

Plate 20: A hurling ball, from St Columb Major, Cornwall, which was won in 1955 by the author's uncle by marriage. Photograph by courtesy of Brian and Susan Bazeley.

Plate 21: Hylton 'Punch' Philipson, wearing his Oxford 'Blue', from an original cartoon, by *Spy* (Sir Leslie Ward, 1851–1922), first published in *Vanity Fair*, on 29th June 1889.

Plate 22: Rose: Josephine Bruce. Photograph by courtesy of Peter Beales Roses.

Plate 23: The famous rose bush, at the head of the grave of Edward FitzGerald, in the churchyard at Boulge, Suffolk. Photograph by courtesy of Laurence Mann.

Plate 24: Rose: Chloris. Photograph by courtesy of JS Storey.

Plate 25: Overview of Villa D'Este, Lake Como. Photograph by courtesy of Villa D'Este.

Plate 26: The Venice-Simplon-Orient Express. Photograph by courtesy of Venice-Simplon-Orient Express.

Plate 27: The 1931 8 litre Bentley, first owned by actor-manager Jack Buchanan. Photograph by courtesy of Martin Daly, of The School Garage.

Plate 28: A motor car mascot, in the form of 'Bonzo', the cartoon dog. Photograph by courtesy of Louis Lejeune Ltd.

Plate 29: Bristol Cars' Bristol Fighter T. Photograph by courtesy of Bristol Cars Ltd.

Plate 30: View of Badrutt's Palace Hotel and the lake, St Moritz. Photograph by courtesy of Badrutt's Palace Hotel.

Plate 31: Ella Shields, as 'Burlington Bertie from Bow', from an original cartoon poster, by Elizabeth Pyke.

CHAPTER 5

Golf, Tennis, Badminton, Squash, Croquet, Fencing, Target Shooting, Bowls

Though the Dutch game of kolf has been claimed as the origin, the first undoubted reference to golf was in 1457 when the Scottish Parliament deplored its popularity, along with that of football, since it took young men away from archery practice.

Oxford Companion to British History

Golf

According to the Appendix to Vol. 1 of Sir William Ouseley's *Travels in Various Countries of the East*, golf bears considerable resemblance to the ancient Royal Persian Game of Chu'ga'n, played for centuries BC and this vies with the Dutch game of kolf as the origin of golf. Apart from the reference to this, in its modern form, this is originally a Scottish game and, so, purists pronounce it 'goff'. Mark Twain (born Samuel Langhorne Clemens 1835–1910) described the game as 'a good walk spoiled' and many a 'golfing widow' has had cause to complain about the game, which often ends with a session in the '*nineteenth hole*'. Blackheath was the first club established in England – that is the first outside Scotland. Some famous British courses are: Wentworth, Walton Heath, Sunningdale, Royal Lytham & St Anne's, Prince's, Royal Cinque Ports, Royal Liverpool, St Andrew's Old Course (the oldest course in the world), Gleneagles, Royal Dornoch, Old Prestwick, Royal Dublin, Royal County Down, Carnoustie, Killarney and Royal St George's, at Sandwich in Kent, which formed the basis for the 'Royal St Mark's' club in Ian Fleming's *Goldfinger*, where Auric Goldfinger and Bond play a round of golf; also the club of which Fleming was captain elect at the time of his death. There are, of course, also wonderful courses and links (a golf club on the coast) in many countries around the world.

Talking of a Scottish game and Ian Fleming, reminds me that he left some indicators of the inspiration for James Bond. Sir Fitzroy Hew Royle MacLean of Dunconnel, 1st Baronet of Strachur and Glensluain, KT, DSO, 15th Keeper and Captain of Dunconnel Castle [also holder of the French Croix de Guerre; Russian Order of Kutuzov and the Yugoslav Order of the Partisan Star] (1911–1996): Scottish diplomat, soldier, explorer, writer and Member of Parliament, was a founding member of the Special Airborne Service (SAS). He led expeditions behind enemy lines, during World War II, and was a leader of the expeditionary force sent to assist Marshal Tito in resisting Nazi advances. Amongst many other things, he wrote *Eastern Approaches* and a biography of Marshall Tito. As *The Daily Telegraph*, dated 18 June 1996 states, he knew Ian Fleming (indeed, since Fleming was born in 1908, their time at Eton must have over-lapped) and Fleming would have been well-versed in his wartime exploits. However, there is another possible template for James Bond: Sir William Stephenson (1897–1989) CC, MC, DFC was a Canadian soldier, airman, inventor and businessman who became the senior officer of British Intelligence in the west, during the Second World War. He was also the first non-American to win the then highest American civilian award, the Presidential Medal for Merit. A controversial book about him, called *A Man Called Intrepid* ('Intrepid' being his wartime code name), was written about him by William Stevenson (no relation), and published by Harcourt in 1976. Whatever else may be said about it, it is a gripping tale. Moreover, on 21st October 1962, Ian Fleming wrote in *The Times*: 'James Bond is a highly romanticized version of a true spy. The real thing is William Stephenson.'

The Royal and Ancient Golf Club is based at St Andrews and is the governing body of golf. It was founded in 1834, in the reign of William IV. From 1754, it had previously been called the Society of St Andrew's Golfers.

I recall that, at the age of about ten, I was given part of a set of cut-down, hickory-shafted golf clubs: including a couple of woods (or drivers), plus irons in numbers one (a *cleek*), three, five (a *mashie*), seven and eight (a *niblick* or *wedge*) as well as a putter (which had belonged to some cousin of my paternal grandfather); a tartan golf bag, a packet of plastic tees and a selection of golf balls: Dunlops and Penfolds (the year 2008, as the centenary of Ian Fleming's birth, saw the re-introduction of the Penfold Hearts golf ball, James Bond's ball of choice).

With my quaint juvenile kit, and after some lessons from a professional, I learned to play really quite well and, for two reasons, might wish that I had become a professional golfer: just think of all that fresh air and cash! On the other hand, I'd have had to have sold my soul to the very devil and allowed the paparazzi into my life. Moreover, there is far too much promotion of professional sport in an age that idolizes (often air-headed) 'sportsmen' who devote their lives to 'careers' in sports that have been turned into Big Business (with all the attendant advertising filth), and the world has clean forgotten that such people were once mildly despised by amateurs. Now even the Olympic Games, once exclusively an amateur competition, have been mired in the money game. In addition to the competition medals and cash spin-offs these 'sporting' men and women are also being given national honours of a high level too, when once competing was done for the love of the game and the honour of representing one's country. Knighting them for winning Olympic gold medals is about as incongruous as superannuated Rockers being offered (and accepting) knighthoods. Sporting activities and games are far better enjoyed for pure recreation; although thorough proficiency should still be the objective and a competitive edge maintained.

Golfing Equipment

MacGregor Golf was founded in 1897, by Edward Canby, in Dayton Ohio, when he converted his shoe last factory into a factory for the manufacture of golf woods. In those days, of course, golf woods were, head and shaft, all made out of wood. They soon started forging irons too and, in fact, it was MacGregor that was the first to introduce steel shafts. Then they became the first to use titanium for the heads of woods. Their ranges of clubs include 'Tourney' woods; 'VIP' irons; Hoylake, Prestwick, and Lytham putters. Nowadays, light graphite shafts are much in favour and there are hosts of makers in the Far East.

MacGregor also manufacture balls and other equipment, such as bags, caps and umbrellas.

As already noted, Penfold Hearts golf balls are available again, through the manufacturer. Choice of both clubs and balls will depend on your level of play. Generally, fatter-headed irons are more suitable for beginners because they are more forgiving of error but you need to go to a golf club professional, have some lessons and ask him to advise you over choice of equipment.

Some golfing terms explained

In 1890, the secretary of Coventry Golf Club thought of standardizing the ground score by which a notional, competent golfer could get around the course. During a competition a player remarked that "this [notional] player of yours is a regular Bogey man!" From this 'Bogey' came to mean what is now called 'Par' for the course. A change came about when American players started using the term 'Bogey' to denote a score of one over par. In 1892 the United

Services' Club at Gosport, in Hampshire, introduced the Bogey score, within the original meaning but the notional player could not be 'Mister' Bogey, as the Club had only servicemen as members, so the Bogey score here was called 'Colonel Bogey'.

'Par for the course' was actually an older expression, dating from 1870 at Prestwick Golf Club; 'par' had originally been a stock exchange expression for regular prices on stocks. However, nationwide introduction of pars for courses and handicapping occurred in the USA before the end of the nineteenth century; whereas it did not happen in Britain until 1925. Now 'Standard Scratch Scores' are regulated by the Golf Unions of the countries where golf is played. A 'handicap' is an allowance of shots given to a player according to his proficiency, so that a scratch player who gets around a course at par has a nil 'handicap' but a male novice will start out with a twenty-four handicap (a female novice starts at thirty-six) – meaning that he will be expected to complete a round of golf, twenty four over par and, accordingly, his actual score is adjusted by deducting the handicap figure from the actual score. The purpose is to enable golfers of different standards to be able to play against each other fairly.

'Birdie' derives from the nineteenth century American term for something good being described as a 'bird'. Near the end of the nineteenth century, three players were playing a par four hole and one player's second ball landed near the hole and he holed his third shot, ending at one under par. One of the others described it as 'a bird of a shot' and the expression 'birdie' soon generally caught on. An 'eagle' is a score of two under par and is just an extension from 'birdie' and the same goes for 'albatross' which is the very rare three under par.

'Fore!' is the expression shouted to other golfers who are at risk of being hit by your ball. It just means "beware to the fore". Of course, you would not deliberately drive a golf ball at anyone (they have been known to kill) but shots can go astray. Plainly, the most important point of golfing etiquette is never to get too close to other players and to give way wherever it seems expedient to do so.

The Rules of Golf

The original thirteen rules of golf were introduced in 1744 for a competition at Leith. Now the rules are settled by the Royal and Ancient in Britain and the US Golf Association. There are two basic systems for deciding the winner of a game; first, there is 'match play', where each hole is a separate competition and the golfer with the fewest shots at the hole, wins the hole, so that the winner of the most holes wins the game and, secondly, there is 'stroke play', where the golfer with the fewest number of strokes around the whole course, wins the game.

Tennis

Anyone for tennis?

The game of tennis arguably originated with the Egyptians – from friezes on Temple walls, where a ball game is depicted. It came to Europe with the Moors and fascinated the monks who called it *la soule*. In the Twelfth and Thirteenth centuries AD it came out of the monasteries and a glove and handle supplanted the bare hand. Balls became made of leather stuffed with bran instead of wood and in the Sixteenth to Eighteenth centuries it was a game much favoured in France where it was called *Jeu de paumme* – palm game. Play was started with the cry '*Tenez*!' It was a favoured game with Royal Courts and 'real tennis' was played off the walls (there is a 'real tennis' court at Hampton Court Palace). There are many clubs and even public courts where recreational tennis may be played. Something of the history of the Wimbledon tennis championships is given in *History of Men's Fashion* and I do not repeat it here.

The most famous rackets and balls are probably produced by Wilson but other top makes include Dunlop and Slazenger.

Badminton

Around the first century AD, a game later called Battledore (ie a paddle) and Shuttlecock, was played in China, Japan and India. A shuttlecock was originally a piece of cork crowned with a circle of feathers. Now they are often made of plastic. In any event there are different speeds of shuttlecock; that is to say speeds at which they fly when hit. By the sixteenth century the game was popular in England and then, in the 1860s the British discovered the game of Poona which was played in India. This was similar to Battledore and Shuttlecock but had the addition of a net between the players. The British took the game of Poona back to Britain where in 1873 it was introduced as a society game at the Duke of Beaufort's estate at Badminton. After that, it became called the 'Badminton game'. In 1877, the Bath Badminton Club was formed and introduced rules. Now the International Badminton Federation has one hundred and fifty member countries and there are also international championships such as the Thomas Cup. Makers of equipment, across a range of prices, include Slazenger, Wilson and Carlton.

Squash

This derives from an earlier game called *Racquets*, which itself derives from the game of Fives, in which the ball is hit against a wall with gloved hands. Racquets was popular in Britain by the eighteenth century. At Harrow School they started using a softer ball which 'squashed' against the wall and did not rebound so fast or predictably. By the 1860s there were purpose-built squash courts at the school. In 1908 there was a Squash sub-committee of the Tennis and Rackets Association. The sport became gradually more popular across the world and, in the 1920s the rules were codified and the Squash Rackets Association was formed in 1928. In the USA there is a similar games called American Hardball, which uses a larger court and slightly different rules: having fifteen point games as opposed to the British game of nine points. Squash equipment is supplied by Wilson, Dunlop, Slazenger and the usual culprits.

Croquet

According to Anthoine Ravez, the president of La Fédération Française de Croquet, the modern game derives from the eleventh century French game called *jeu de mail* and was brought to Britain in the thirteenth century, where the Scots made golf out of it and the Irish created croquet. He goes on to claim that Louis XIV took the game indoors, one rainy day, and gave the world billiards! Whatever one makes of all that, it seems clear that a croquet-like game was known as *pell mell* or *pall mall* in Britain from an early time and, indeed, the central London thoroughfare 'Pall Mall' is named after the game which had been played there, and, even though it might sound unbearably affected to modern British ears, an alternative pronunciation of the street is still 'Pell Mell'. There is association croquet, with its tournaments as well as garden croquet, played by all generations of the same family, to

> *'The moan of doves in immemorial elms,*
> *And the murmuring of innumerable bees.'*

and nicely punctuated by afternoon tea. The association croquet is governed by Croquet Associations for the various countries where it is played and they also have equipment for sale; from whole croquet sets to mallets and balls. There are basic laws and rules too for association and garden types of the game and for those interested, Colonel Pritchard's book, mentioned in the Bibliography, is a good starting point, before the play begins.

Fencing

Having already mentioned that it would be as easy to learn to fish as to fence from a book, I shall keep this section relatively brief. Fencing has been practised since ancient times and (along with several other activities that I have remarked in the course of these three books), the Egyptians were certainly on to it. In Europe there was jousting and tournament combat (with broadswords), in the Middle Ages. Modern fencing derives from the unarmoured duelling, with rapiers, from the sixteenth century. These rapiers were edged weapons but the main attack was made with them by the thrust. This type of duelling began in Spain and Italy and spread to north-west Europe. By the eighteenth century the rapier had become a shorter and lighter sword which was popularized in France. It was buttoned with a flower-like leather safety button and the sword became known as 'le fleuret'; in England it was called the foil. The French school of fencing is the basis of the modern method.

The foil gave rise, in turn to the development of the unedged *epée de terrain*.

Cutting swords had been used in backsword prize fights to about the seventeenth century and broadswords, sabres and cutlasses remained the favoured weapons of naval and military men; although sabres developed into the lighter modern weapons. Italian and German schools came to dominate the technique for sabre fighting. Sword duels were fought in Europe over sporting disputes as late as the 1920s and might even still occur; although they are unlikely to attract publicity. However, according to various news reports: in 1997, the mayor of Calabria, in Italy, publicly challenged certain Mafiosi to a sword duel! There are events for the foil, sabre and epée in the Olympic Games.

Fencing Schools

There are fencing schools all over the world. The London Fencing Club is an example and it offers beginners' courses for all ages. Additionally, certain sporting clubs, such as the Lansdowne Club (again in London), provide tuition and facilities for members.

Target Shooting

This sport has been affected by the UK guns laws; since, generally, pistols (except some antique pieces and certain air pistols), and revolvers may not be lawfully held in a useable condition. However, there is still rifle target shooting, such as that arranged through the National Rifle Association of the UK and some clubs exist that organize air gun events. So far as 'plinking' is concerned, that is to say *ad hoc* air gun target practice on cans and so forth in the back garden: there are even now strict laws on this exercise and it is probably best to join a local air gun club, which will organize safe and lawful exercises, to ensure that your collar is not felt by Mr Policeman. In any event, always bear in mind that air guns *are* potentially lethal weapons and, therefore, the comments on gun safety, earlier in this book, apply as much to air guns as to any other guns.

Archery

Evidence of arrows in Somerset from around 2000 BC has been found but it was after the Battle of Hastings that long-bow development and skills became highly refined. Indeed, such was the perceived importance of practice that there were periodic bans on golf, football and bowls because they were distractions from archery practice. Even with the development of firearms from the fifteenth century there remained many with an enthusiasm for the sport of archery and target archery was developed from the seventeenth century and The Society of Archers was founded at Scorton in 1673, and still holds an annual tournament for the Silver Arrow. The Royal Company of Archers was established in 1676; The (Royal) Toxophilite Society in 1781; The Woodmen of Arden in 1785; The Royal British Bowmen in 1787. Grand National Archery meetings began at York in 1844 and The Grand National Archery Society (now called Archery GB) was founded in Liverpool in 1861 and now controls the sport in Britain and is a source of information about local clubs, equipment and events.

Bowls

Famously, according to Sir Francis Drake, when told, during a game of bowls on Plymouth Hoe, of the advance of the Spanish Armada:

'There is time to finish the game and to thrash the Spaniards too.'

perfectly demonstrating, in the glorious result (even if, as legend has it, he lost the bowls' match), that this ancient game is not just for older men. There is possibly a link between bowls and the ancient Egyptian game of skittles. The Romans had their '*bocci*' and other ancient people also threw round objects, including stones, at targets. The oldest bowling green, in current use, is in Southampton and dates from 1299. Early British laws tried to ban it as a game as (like golf), it tended to distract men from archery practice. Legislation in force between 1541 and 1845 allowed play only at Christmas, except for those who could run to the hundred pound general licence fee! Biased bowls (essential to the modern game, with its swerving trajectory), were introduced in 1522 and the 'Jack' as the target ball was a seventeenth century introduction. Bowls were, until recently, made out of *Lignum vitae*, a wood so dense that it sinks in water.

However, modern technology has produced bowls made out of synthetic material which are even less susceptible to climactic conditions in their use.

At a meeting of various British clubs in Glasgow in 1848 there was standardization of the laws of the game and the Scottish Bowling Association was formed in 1892; followed by the English Bowling Association in 1903, and the International Bowling Association in 1905. Most places have a bowling club, which should be approached by those interested, and they will have lists of local stockists of bowls and cases.

CHAPTER 6

Town and Country Living

'Better beans and bacon in peace than cakes and ale in fear.'

From Town Mouse and Country Mouse
Aesop's Fables

Introduction

Of course living in the countryside need not be humble and living in the town need not be that dangerous, even if it is not as safe as the countryside. However, as I mention in the Introduction to this book, town and country are, these days, very different places and, I suspect that there is little understanding between people who spend most of their lives in the town and those who spend their lives in the country. This is a great pity because misunderstanding breeds fear and fear, more often than not, breeds aggression; in the same way that *Town and Gown* antipathy can emerge in cities that harbour universities. The misunderstandings between town and country can lead to senseless decisions by Parliament, such as that to legislate (or at least to *attempt* to legislate) to ban 'hunting with dogs'. It is senseless and inconsistent too. It is senseless primarily in that the legislation aims to put the interests of a particular species of vermin, the fox (which needs to be controlled anyway), ahead of the interests of the human beings actually employed for the purpose of hunting and also ahead of the lives of the thousands of hounds, which are hunting, pack creatures and cannot, apart from the little Beagle, be successfully kept as pets. That argument is quite beside the argument that hunting with hounds is a tradition from time immemorial in Britain (and many other countries, dating from early mankind), which should not lightly be disturbed by our patronizing, hyper-sensitive, soft and soppy *know-all* generation. It is plainly *inconsistent* in its intention because the hunting of rabbits (which could not possibly outrun a pack of hounds) is *permitted as expressly exempt hunting*, whereas the hare (which certainly can gracefully outrun the hounds, as well as the different dogs used for hare coursing), is protected!

The point of this observation is not just to seize any old excuse to discharge a rant about the *state of the nation* (which, frankly, could be much better), but to make the point that, if town people spent a reasonable proportion of their time in country communities and country people went to town regularly, there would be less misunderstanding and so, less fear and aggression and, instead, greater application of the aphorism:

'Live and let live'

but applied, as it should be: between human beings; in some recognition of the spirit of Alexander Pope's fine lines:

'Know then thyself, presume not God to scan;
The proper study of mankind is man.'

Housing – Town & Country and important features

So long as you remain a bachelor, you do not really need to live outside the *gods' quad* (as defined in *History of Men's Fashion*), and you may easily rely upon family and friends or hotels and inns for accommodation out of town. Afterwards, in due course, you are likely to find yourself: across in Kensington, Chelsea, St John's Wood or Little Venice; up in the hills of Highgate; Hampstead or Muswell Hill; over the river in Greenwich, Blackheath Village, Dulwich, Twickenham or Richmond, or even beetling in from the *far side* of Tenterden, Tunbridge Wells, Tonbridge, Hertford, Hatfield or Hitchin, with an estate car, folding baby buggies and a standing appointment at the nearest Waitrose and a farmers' market on Saturday mornings – but there is plenty of time for all that.

Town living

There are flats, often (but not just), of the *compact* kind in the streets in and around Jermyn Street; St James's Square and on and around, Piccadilly; even in St James's Street itself. These have never come cheap but there are obvious savings, in time and money and even patience, against travelling in to town from the Styx.

St James's Square: one of London's first 'garden squares' of houses; originally built from 1662, on land held by Henry Jermyn, 1st Earl of St Albans (hence, of course, Jermyn Street), for courtiers, who needed to be near Whitehall and St James's Palaces. It is still, for many, the centre of the Metropolis (for some, it is the centre of the Universe itself), and remains the only garden square in the parish of St James's. In fact, the gardens form nearly a circle and contain some fine London Plane trees, a beautiful ornamental cherry tree, commemorating

WPC Yvonne Fletcher, tragically shot dead in the Libyan Embassy siege, in the north-east corner of the square in 1984, and an equestrian statue (dated 1808) of 'King Billy' – William III (1650–1702, reigned 1689–1702, with Queen Mary until her death in 1694); he died in a fall from his horse when it fell in a molehill, which is represented on the statue. There is also a fairly recent sculpture of a stag (by the sculptor Marcus Cornish), which has been introduced into the south-west corner.

At first, there had been a pond in the middle of the Square. Some of the original houses remain on the north and north-eastern sides. The Naval and Military Club (the 'In and Out' – from the signs painted on the gate posts at the club's former address at 94 Piccadilly) occupies the Astors' former town house in the north east corner (which bears a blue commemorative plaque to Nancy Astor). The London Library is up in the north-west corner, near the East India Club and there is another interesting blue commemorative plaque on number 12; to Ada, Countess of Lovelace (1815–1852), who is described as the 'first computer programmer' (of Charles Babbage's difference and analytical engines).

The southern side of the square was not originally developed and had been just a rubbish dump but was later developed with smaller houses, fronting not onto the Square – but onto Pall Mall (the first street in London to be lit by gas, as early as 1807). The name 'Pall Mall' derives, as already noted, from *Pell Mell* – a ball game once played there. As a matter of interest, the first house in the world to be lit by gas lighting was the house of Scottish engineer William Murdoch, who installed it in his house in Redruth, Cornwall, around 1790.

Now the southern side of St James's Square is a fairly modern (and externally unprepossessing) office block, in the brutalist architectural style, with penthouse flats on the top – whose occupants enjoy equal access, with the others in the Square, to the private gardens even when they are locked to the public. You need to apply to the Trustees of the Square to obtain a key and there is a small charge. Some good agents for this area are: Michael Graham, of Pall Mall, and Knight Frank in Mount Street.

If you are interested in a set of chambers in Albany, opposite Fortnum & Mason in Piccadilly, just ask the porters about applying to the trustees. The quite magnificent main entrance to the building is set back from the road and easy to miss unless you stop and look up at it. The building and gardens (including the long, covered 'Ropewalk') stretch right back to Vigo Street, where there is a discreet back door in the wall. The original building was built in 1770 for the first Lord Melbourne who was persuaded, in 1793, to swap the house for another in Whitehall to oblige the then Duke of York, who wished to live there. Eight years later it was sold to repay the mortgages of banker Thomas Coutts.

It was then decided to divide the building up into bachelor apartments, in which a whole host of the Great, the Good and the Very Bad have lived, such as: Henry Holland (architect); Lord Brougham (main Counsel for Queen Caroline in her trial before the House of Lords in the passage of the Pains and Penalties Bill 1820, by which George IV tried (unsuccessfully in the result) to divorce her for adultery); Lord Palmerston (politician and sometime Prime Minister, often remembered for his famous speech *Civis Romanus sum* ('I am a Roman citizen') in defence of his decision to send British naval ships to protect Don Pacifico (despite his name, a Jewish British subject) from the predations of anti-semites in Athens; remembered too for jumping into the *wrong bed* at various country houses); George Canning, another sometime Prime Minister; Lord Byron, poet and international rascal (who smuggled the second Lord Melbourne's wife, Lady Caroline Lamb, into his chambers in Albany dressed as a page boy); writers J B Priestley and Terence Rattigan, and more modern politicians Edward Heath and Alan Clark (who is supposed to have entertained his 'coven', comprising the wife and two daughters of a South African Judge, in his rooms there).

Maybe the most advantageously positioned British fictional hero's apartment was that of Dorothy L Sayers sleuthing hero Lord Peter Wimsey, at 110A Piccadilly, opposite Green Park: for my money it beats James Bond's pad in Chelsea and Sherlock Holmes's flat at 221B Baker Street. According to her friend and biographer, Barbara Reynolds, Sayers actually invented Wimsey and had him living in Piccadilly, in an unpublished spoof Sexton Blake story that she wrote while recovering from mumps in France in late 1919 or early 1920; that is long before the first Wimsey novel appeared: *Whose Body?* in 1923.

Mentioning Dorothy L Sayers (who lived for years in Bloomsbury), has reminded me that there are other seldom considered residential enclaves in central London, which are worth considering in your bachelor days; all are reasonably close to the gods' quad but with property that is less expensive than that within it, or the other nearby districts of Covent Garden and Soho.

The first is Bloomsbury, which (although it has no official borders), stretches, roughly, from the Euston Road in the north to Holborn and New Oxford Street in the south and from Gray's Inn Road in the east to Tottenham Court Road in the west (some say that it stops at Gower Street in the west). It is the area of London that I came to know very well as it harbours my *alma mater* 'The Godless Institution of Gower Street' (University College, London which, unlike Oxford and Cambridge Universities, was founded (in 1826), without any requirement for graduation to depend upon a willingness to subscribe to the 39 Articles of Religion of the Church of England and which admitted women on equal terms with men from the outset).

There are lovely garden squares: Bloomsbury Square, similar to a diminutive St James's Square, is in fact a circle and, laid out by the Earl of Southampton, it dates from the same time; Russell Square, Gordon Square, Woburn Square; Torrington Square; Tavistock Square; Mecklenburgh Square; Brunswick Square; Queen's Square, and Cartwright Gardens. Most of the development was the result of the activities of the Russell family of the Dukes of Bedford: hence the names of many of the squares and streets, deriving from their family name; their estates and titles. Moreover, there are many hidden gems such as Woburn Walk off Upper Woburn Place, which is a delightful pedestrian alley lined with shops and restaurants with flats over them. A commemorative plaque tells us that the great poet W B Yeats lived in one of them in his younger days and, of course, the area is awash with memorials and memories of the literary Bloomsbury Group (not to mention Charles Dickens, the historian R H Tawney and Dorothy L Sayers) as well as having there many academic institutions and teaching hospital establishments and the British Museum are also to be found there. London University's Senate House in Malet Street (strongly redolent of Nazi architecture, I always think), is where John Betjeman met the real Miss Joan Hunter Dunne, during her war work in the building, in the Second World War, and where he asked her to lunch so that he could present her (fortunately to her delight), with one of my favourite Betjeman poems: *A Subaltern's Love Song*, which begins:

'Miss J Hunter Dunne, Miss J Hunter Dunne,
Furnish'd and burnish'd by Aldershot sun...'

Besides all that, Bloomsbury is within easy walking distance of every place in central London that any fellow could wish to visit. Useful agents which cover sales and lettings in this area are Hudsons Property and Winkworth & Co.

The next area is Fitzrovia, named after Fitzroy Square, Fitzroy Street and the Fitzroy Tavern. Its exact boundaries have been a subject of some debate but let us say, for the sake of argument (and accepting that there might be possible overlaps with Bloomsbury) that Fitzrovia stretches from the Euston Road in the north to Oxford Street in the south and between Tottenham Court Road in the east to Great Portland Street in the west. Some people put Gower Street as the eastern border and take out the area around Bloomsbury Square. Development was started here by Charles Fitzroy, later Lord Southampton, in the eighteenth century. From his family some of the street names derive but the Devonshire and Portland families also owned land here and developed it, accounting for the presence of their names as the names of other thoroughfares. The biggest developments here were the BT Tower (formerly the 'Post Office Tower') and the old Middlesex Hospital, the site of which is about to be redeveloped. We hold our breath and pray. The area has a history of bohemianism, having housed and watered (at various times) characters as diverse as Virginia Woolf and Jimi Hendrix; Dylan Thomas and Aleister Crowley (an occultist known as 'The Beast'); George Orwell and Augustus John and a host of others. Apart from the Fitzroy Tavern, another well-known pub here is the Newman Arms.

The property in this area includes some splendid mansion flats. Useful agents which cover sales and lettings in this area are: Richard James (lettings); Hudsons Property, and Bairstoweves.

There is also Clerkenwell, to the north-east of Bloomsbury but I have always found this to be a rather gloomy area with a pregnant, brooding atmosphere, which I find disagreeable, and so I omit discussion of it.

Finally, in my choices, there is the Barbican development, which includes residential accommodation, if you happen to like architecture in the brutalist School. The Barbican (which means 'fortification') dates back to Roman times and it was they who fortified it. Always a cosmopolitan, even bohemian area, Shakespeare lived, for a time, on the corner of Monkwell and Silver Streets and its small-time 'Grub Street writers' have given the language a colourful, descriptive phrase. The Great Plague of 1665 decimated the population and the Great Fire of the following year reached as far as Smithfield. What was left gradually decayed until the Nazi's Blitzed it and all was rubble.

It was not until 1955 that first proposals were put to redevelop the bombsite and not until 1971 that building began, and it was not until 1982 that the Barbican Centre (the last part of the development) was opened. This is a performing arts complex and is home to the London Symphony Orchestra and the BBC Symphony Orchestra, as well as housing restaurants, conference facilities, trade exhibition halls and a public library. Agents Hurford, Salvi, Carr specialise in sales and lettings in this area.

Country living

There are two main kinds of country living: there is committed country living and there is weekend and holiday country living. If you are going to be a committed country dweller and well and truly get mud on your boots, you can choose to live just about anywhere you please. However, if you are a weekender-pretender, you will probably want to be within striking distance of London or one of the other towns or cities to make travelling to and fro' worthwhile; although I do know one family of weekender-pretenders who travel from Middlesex to a cottage in mid-Wales at the drop of a hat but they are just as likely to jump in the car, at a moment's notice, and nip over to Lake Constance.

Of course, most people are born to town or country and, except where education or work takes them away, exercise little choice over where they end up. However, for those who do exercise choice in the matter, there are still many relatively unspoiled cities, towns and villages around London and other large conurbations. Those around London, for my money would include: St Albans and Hertford in Hertfordshire; Princes Risborough and Buckingham in Buckinghamshire; Witham and Colchester in Essex; Sandwich and Tenterden in Kent; Camberley and Reigate in Surrey; Brighton and Rye in East Sussex, and Chichester, Hassock and Hove in West Sussex.

If you have it in mind to rent a property in the countryside, it is well worth bearing in mind that the National Trust lets some of its properties, both on short-term and long-term bases, provided that you are prepared to allow public access, at certain times, for viewing.

Some thoughts on dressing in town and country, at home and abroad; some expressions and some additional useful items of clothing

Some further thoughts on dress in town

One of the reviewers of *History of Men's Fashion* applauded the fact that I was '*crisp*' on 'brown in town' and, for myself, I maintain my general position. However, some have pointed out that there is room for *rus in urbe* and that it is preferable to some of the modern alternatives. Plainly, the rules described in *History of Men's Fashion* (which need to be *known* if they are to be broken with panache), are more relaxed if you are going to a museum, shopping, or to feed the pelicans in the park than if you are going to deliver a lecture at the Royal Geographical Society, a meeting or conference with professional advisers or lunch at your club. Certainly, the adoption of a smart version of *rus in urbe*, say, a nicely set-off, restrained tweed suit, is far preferable for *leisure time* in town, to the widespread adoption of jumpers and jeans and similar casual clothes (even track suits), which sit uneasily with the essential opulence and decorum of the centre of London, or any of the world's great cities.

I know that there is a significant contingent of men who rail at observance of *any* 'rules' for dress (or, possibly, for anything much) but they have yet to realize that human society would wither on the vine without recognition of a certain irreducible minimum of customs. By this I mean customary rules, which carry only social sanctions. One of these is an observance of the usual regulation of black tie and dinner jackets. To my mind, observance of the customary combinations enhances the cohesiveness of our civilization and the encouragement of certain fashion and style advisers merely to give a nod to custom and pitch up in something like a dinner jacket, shirt open to the navel, jeans and velvet slippers (and, probably, no socks) or even just to wear an evening scarf with a suit and open-necked shirt to an occasion calling for 'black tie' suggests to me that they are not so much giving a nod to custom as they are cocking a snook at custom as well as at all those who choose to observe custom. I deprecate their self-appointed proclamations, calling for the further dilution of the little that is left of ceremony and custom in our modern world. I know that this is the age of the common man but we do not all have to become converts to his tastes, do we? Having said that, I have already mentioned in *History of Men's Fashion* that the main precursor of the ordinary four-in-hand day tie was originally an invention as an unusual form of evening tie and, sometimes, at 'celebrity' events, these ties in black are worn with a dinner jacket.

However, the plain fact of the matter is that the world is growing ever less formal. King Edward VII (although a stickler for correct Court dress), had abandoned morning dress for Newmarket and Goodwood and George V abandoned morning dress for the Chelsea Flower Show. Certainly, by a point somewhere near the end of the First World War, frock and morning coats were not regularly worn by many in the City anymore and, as one of his first acts as king, King Edward VIII finished the process that his grandfather and father had started and abolished the frock coat for wear at Court, since he preferred lounge suits. Professionals, bankers and businessmen (even in provincial towns) adopted a short black, ventless coat (known in the USA and some other places as a 'stroller'), matching vest and black and white, Cashmere-striped (spongebag) trousers; together with a white shirt, stiff collar, sombre tie; black coke (bowler), Cambridge (square-crowned coke), or homburg hat, chamois gloves and a tightly-rolled umbrella, as an echo of morning dress. Remember the civilian dress of bank manager Captain Mainwaring and his clerk Sergeant Wilson in Jimmy Perry and David Croft's delightful television series *Dad's Army*?

With such a rig, Churchill normally stuck to the gold-topped, malacca cane that he had inherited from his wife's brother. The short coat was most often single-breasted, with either double-breasted or step lapels and plain, jetted pockets with no flaps. However, even the adoption of this degree of dilution of formality has fallen into desuetude; except for some managers in the hotel and catering industry. Now the generally accepted city professional and business suit is a dark woollen worsted suit; although the less formal flannel (particularly in broad, 'banker', chalk-stripes) has found a place too. So far as shirts are concerned, in a fairly recent article in *The Times*, Michael Gove MP stated that the 'über-posh' don't wear white shirts but cream ones. In fact, it is interesting to learn that the French shirtmaker Charvet proudly offers a choice of around *four hundred shades of white*! My own favourite choices for town shirts are: plain white, cream and pale blue. I salute those who have the time and patience to match up patterned shirts and ties but, to my mind, *ars longa tempus fugit*, and I don't find the time for it.

Some expressions related to dressing

'Dressed to the nines': means dressed superlatively well for the occasion. It is of uncertain derivation and several theories have been advanced. It seems that 'to the nines' was previously used as a general expression of approval; for example see William Hamilton's Epistle to Ramsay of 1719: 'How to the nines they did content me' and in the lines by Robbie Burns:

> 'Thou paints auld Nature to the nines,
> In thy sweet Caledonian lines...'

One plausible explanation for the use of this phrase, in relation to dress, is that the 99th Regiment of Foot was sartorially an extremely smart Regiment and other Regiments tried to emulate the superlative '9s'. Nine has always been seen as a special number and, to start with, nine is the largest primary number and any number multiplied by nine produces a figure which combines primary numbers that add up to nine (e.g. nine multiplied by nine equals eighty-one and eight plus one equals nine). Moreover, there were the Nine Muses (Calliope, chief Muse and Muse of epic poetry; Euterpe, Muse of lyric song; Clio, Muse of history; Erato, Muse of erotic poetry; Thelpomene, Muse of tragedy; Polyhymnia, Muse of sacred song; Tersichore, Muse of dance; Thalia, Muse of comedy and Urania, Muse of astronomy). There were also the Nine Worthies of the ancient world (Joshua, David, Judas, Maccabaeus, Hector, Alexander, Julius Caesar, Charlemagne and Godfrey of Bouillon). A modern phrase denoting happiness is 'being on cloud nine'.

One might also strive to be the 'bee's knees' or the 'cat's whiskers' – but one would probably avoid being the 'dog's bollocks' – except, possibly, in an unmixed sporting field. All these last phrases seem to be of twentieth century slang origin, as is 'dressed to kill': another slang phrase meaning dressed to astonish and, maybe, *to seduce*. 'Dressed (or done) up like a dog's dinner' means looking over-dressed for the occasion or ill at ease in formal clothes and 'mutton dressed as lamb' means being dressed in clothes that are too young for one's years. An over-dressed man, especially a young man, might be called a 'popinjay' (an ornamental representation of a parrot on a tapestry or in a painting), or hear *sotto voce* the words *'Do you suppose that he's on the stage?'*

A little more on blazers and reefers

A blazer is, strictly, a single-breasted jacket, mainly associated with schools, colleges and sports' clubs and made in their colours – often in stripes and often has patch pockets and club buttons. The reefer jacket is a double-breasted jacket in a naval style and normally navy blue, with unflapped jetted side pockets; although this style in a lounge coat is also, technically, a 'reefer'. However, in fact, both blazer and reefer are associated with summer dress and so (to my mind), they match better with white flannels or ducks and white buckskin or co-respondent (spectator) shoes than they do with grey flannels and brown or oxblood brogues, with which they seem (probably out of practical considerations), to be increasingly paired. When I first made this point in *History of Men's Fashion* I attracted a degree of criticism, from certain quarters, which has since been quietly replaced by a seeming resurgence in the manufacture of co-respondent shoes and white flannels!

Panama hats

Obviously, a consistent weave and solid light colour are highly desirable and some people count the rings inside the crown (*vueltas*); the more the better. Brent Black Panamas stock includes exhibition quality versions; each costing a small fortune – even up to tens of thousands of dollars for one hat. They have one in production at the moment, called 'The Hat', which is rumoured to carry a price tag of up to one hundred thousand dollars. 'Where did you get *that hat*?' – answer – from Simón Espinal, of Ecuador, said, by Brent Black, to be the best panama hat weaver in the world. 'The Hat' will take five months to make. His hats, available through Brent Black, normally *start* at four thousand dollars. A famous early example of one of the best quality hats of a former age was presented to Emperor Napoleon III at the Paris Exhibition in 1855. I have recently also learned of the firm of panamas.biz

Boaters

The hatter James Lock says that the modern version of the straw boater (made of sennit straw plait), derives from the nineteenth century hats worn by midshipmen in the Royal Navy. They are normally sold with plain black bands but it is perfectly correct to wear these with hatbands in the colours of your school, college or boat club.

CHAPTER 7

Country Activities and Wine Cellars

'Town and country do your best for in this parish I must rest.

Words that traditionally accompany the
throwing up of the St Columb hurling ball

Building a night-scented garden

Come into the garden, Maud,
For the black bat night has flown,
Come into the garden, Maud,
I am here at the gate alone.
And the woodbine spices are wafted abroad,
And the musk of the rose is blown.

Alfred, Lord Tennyson

A night-scented garden can be virtually any size and, even if you are an apartment dweller, you could still have window boxes and hanging baskets, for the smaller plants. Some ideas for the plants include violets (*Viola odorata*) of which there are many varieties, available from Groves Nurseries and the Devon Violet Nursery; the white varieties of *Nicotiana* (the tobacco plant); Colchester White (*Centaurea*); Four o'clock Alba (*Pisonia alba*); Night-scented Stock (*Matthiola longipetala*); Night-blooming Jasmine (*Jasminum cestrum nocturnum*); Iris Pippa Sandford; Angel's Trumpet of the genus *Datura* and, during warm seasons, certain Gardenias such as *Gardenia Jasminoides*; not to forget Woodbine or honeysuckle (*Lonicera periclymenum*). Gently sprinkling the plants with water, after sunset, will help to release the fragrances.

As well as a night-scented garden, you might also like to consider in the ordinary course of things, combining, over a pergola, a sturdy, climbing, scented Bourbon rose, such as *Kathleen Harrop,* or a scented Wichurana rambler, such as *Albertine*, with summer jasmine (*jasminum officinale*) and winter jasmine (*jasminum polyanthus*), for show and scent. Of course, if you want to attract butterflies, you must have a 'butterfly bush' and *Buddleia davidii* is a good one.

Building a herb garden

And God said, Behold, I have given you every herb-bearing seed, which is upon the face of the earth…

Genesis 1:29

There is every reason why a full-size night-scented garden should be close to an aromatic herb garden, where might be grown to advantage any of the following main herbs, in sunny beds (of good fertile soil), traditionally separated by clipped box hedges. Remember that anything that has a pharmacological effect on the body is a drug and herbs have been used as medicines for centuries. Therefore, take care if you think of mixing herbal remedies with prescription medicines and preferably seek your doctor's advice first.

Arnica (*Arnica montana*) – made into an ointment, this helps with chilblains and bruises.

Basil (*Ocimum basilicum*) – is a famous constituent of pesto sauce and the leaves are delicious laid over a simple, true pizza.

Borrage (*Borago officinalis*) – chopped leaves may be used in green salads and can be used to make tea or mixed in punch. It is also useful as a heart tonic.

Chamomile (*Matricaria chamomilla*) – is most famous as a soothing tea infusion and as a sunburn ointment. Sometimes it is planted as an aromatic lawn and exudes its fragrance most when walked over in the twilight.

Chervil (*Anthriscus cereioiium*) – used as a tea it cleans the blood and lowers blood pressure, and is very pleasant as a garnish for fish.

Chives (*Alium schoenoprasum*) – finely chopped, these make a fine component of a green salad and are used to flavour double Double Gloucester cheese to make the splendid Cotswold cheese.

Coriander (*Coriandrum sativum*) – the fresh leaves are often sprinkled over curries just before they are served and the seeds also find culinary uses in Indian cooking.

Curry leaf (*Murraya Koenigii*) – unsurprisingly, this is often used in curries.

Dill (*Anethum graveoleus*) – the leaves and seeds aid digestion and dill is often used in a sauce eaten with smoked salmon and as an essential ingredient of Gravadlax.

Fennel (*Foeniculum vulgare*) – is often used to flavour fish dishes.

Feverfew (*Chrysanthemum parthenium*) – as a tea infusion it can be a great grease-buster and a laxative.

Garlic (*Allium sativum*) – this is a famed culinary herb which needs little introduction. It is another important ingredient of pesto and has blood-cleaning and antibiotic qualities.

Horse radish (*Cochlearia armoracia*) – beloved as a spicy, cold, creamy sauce with hot or cold roast beef and also with smoked salmon. If you are having cold roast beef, make sure that it is thinly sliced and served up with horseradish sauce and Cos lettuce.

Hyssop (*Hyssopus officinalis*) – can be added in small quantities to green salads. Its extract is also used in perfumery and used to colour green Chartreuse and Absinthe.

Lavender (*Lavendula officinalis*) – is famously grown for its oil, which finds uses in perfumery and flower heads are sewn into cloth sachets to act as as a moth-repellent.

Lemon balm (*Melissa officinalis*) – is relaxing as a tea infusion and the leaves may also be added to green salads or fresh fruit, or used to flavour fish.

Lemon verbena (*Aloysia triphylla*) – rub the rough, nearly sticky leaves and smell the lemon scent. This can be made into a relaxing tea and the dried leaves also retain their scent for quite some time and are often used in *potpourri*.

Lovage (*Levisticum officinale*) – this herb is used in an elixir called 'lovage'. The fresh leaves can be used to garnish soups and similar dishes or added to green salads.

Marjoram (*Origanum majorana*) – add the chopped leaves to sauces and soups at the end of cooking.

Mint (*Mentha spicata*) – can be used for anything from making a mint julep to mint sauce to go with lamb cutlets: chop the mint finely and muddle with a little vinegar and a teaspoon of castor sugar.

Oregano (*Oreganum vulgara*) – is similar to marjoram in its uses but it has a stronger flavour; it can usefully liven up scrambled eggs or a plain omelette.

Parsley (*Petroselinum crispum*) – is a well-known herb that is a favourite in creamy sauces with fish, sprinkled over potatoes or mixed with yoghurt as a dressing.

Rocket (*Eruca sativa*) – is delicious as a salad, even on its own.

Rosemary (*Rosmarinus officinalis*) – is most famously teamed up with roast lamb.

Rue (*Ruta graveoteus*) – may be taken as a tea infusion.

Sage (*Salvia officinalis*) – is most widely known as a component of sage and onion stuffing for poultry.

Sorrel (*Rumex acetosa*) – this can be made into sauces that match up well with salmon and pork.

Tarragon (*Artemesia dracunculus*) – use this in vinegar, herb butter, marinades and with eggs and vegetables.

Thyme (*Thymus vulgaris*) – is another herb that complements roast lamb.

Valerian (*Valeriana officinalis*) – the root of this herb can be used in soups and stews and it is also a noted anti-depressant.

Wormwood (*Artemisia absinthum*) – this is most famously included in the notorious drink Absinthe.

Yarrow (*Achillea millefolium*) – applying the leaves to a fresh minor wound or to a nose bleed will help to stop bleeding.

You sow the seeds in trays indoors in accordance with the instructions on the packets and bring them on until sturdy seedlings have grown up an inch or two and then plant them out in well-drained soil, once all risk of frost has passed, and gently water them in.

Roses and rose gardens

> 'Look to the blowing Rose about us – "Lo,
> Laughing," she says, "into the world I blow,
> At once the silken tassel of my Purse
> Tear, and its Treasure on the Garden throw".'

From the translation of the *Rubáiyat of Omar Khayyám*,
by Edward FitzGerald

Everyone with a little land should have a rose garden. It is even possible to achieve one on a terrace, balcony or verandah.

Ancient people loved roses as much as we do and even used the rose in symbolism too. Roses have been found in Egyptian tombs and even in thirty-five million year old fossils in Colorado. The ancient Chinese, the Persians, the Romans and the Greeks (to name a few), were all very fond of roses; Confucius recorded the roses grown in the Chinese Imperial Rose Garden (China roses famously flower repeatedly in the same season) and roses were probably first cultivated in Asia and Arabia some five thousand years ago.

The Greek myth is that Chloris (in Latin Flora), the goddess of flowers, created the first rose out of a dying wood nymph and then asked Aphrodite to give the rose beauty; Dionysius to give her nectar for scent and the Three Graces to give her Charm, Brightness and Joy. Then Zephyr, the West Wind, blew the clouds away and Apollo shone upon the rose and she bloomed. There is still an old garden variety of rose, called Chloris. However, a different Roman myth holds that a beautiful maiden, named Rhodanthe, was exhausted by the importunities of her suitors and found refuge in the Temple of Diana but Diana became jealous of her and so, when her suitors came beating on the doors of the Temple, Diana turned Rhodanthe into the first rose and her suitors into rose thorns.

The rose was the flower most beloved of the goddess Aphrodite and she even turned white roses red with her blood, as she scratched herself on rose thorns hastening to the mortally wounded Adonis; giving mortals the ever-enduring and universal lovers' symbol. According to Homer's *Iliad*, Achilles' shield was partly decorated with garlands, probably of roses and, when Hector fell victim to Achilles' spear, at Troy, his body was anointed with rose oil. Some societies claim that The Christ's Crown of Thorns was made of rose briar and the first *rosaries* were strings of one hundred and fifty dried roses.

Alexander the Great brought many roses back to Europe from the East and the Romans introduced the dog rose (*rosa canina*) to Britain. The rose is famously a symbol of England. The red rose of Lancaster is *Rosa gallica officinalis* and the white rose of York is *Rosa alba*; by legend, they were first plucked, as symbols of opposing forces of Lancaster and York, in Middle Temple Gardens, between Fleet Street and what is now the Thames Embankment. After the Hundred Years' War, between the Houses of Lancaster and York, Lancastrian Henry VII married Elizabeth of York and combined the two roses in the symbolic Tudor rose. There is also the very alluring crimson and white streaked *Rosa mundi* 'Rose of the World'.

Of course, Shakespeare gave us the famous lines of Juliet Capulet bemoaning Romeo Montague's family name, and then concluding:

'What's in a name? That which we call a rose
By any other name would smell as sweet...'

Roses (especially tea rose buds) can make beautiful buttonholes and, on St George's Day (April 23), they used to be worn in every Englishman's hatband. Some men, such as Douglas Fairbanks Jr used to have an artificial carnation to sport when a fresh real one was not available. However, it seems to me that fresh real flowers, whether in a buttonhole or a vase, mark the passing moment with their evanescence; whereas, displaying artificial flowers is an empty gesture and, in every sense, utter vanity.

Happily, São Jorge (symbolized exactly as he is in England, in Benedetto Pistrucci's famous engraving, mounted on horseback slaying the dragon), is also the Patron Saint of Rio de Janeiro and, perhaps, this is why, despite the tropical climate, roses grow here too. It is thought that tea roses were brought to the west, from China, by the tea clippers.

By 1200 AD there were five distinct groups: Damask roses, Alba roses, Centifolia roses, Gallica roses and Scots roses. Gradually increasing hybridization has produced many different varieties. Even as war raged around Europe, Napoleon's Empress Josephine famously encouraged this process in her rose gardens at the Château de Malmaison, where Pierre Joseph Redouté painted his famous collection of watercolours entitled '*Les Roses*'. There was even an instance when the British navy gave safe passage for a French cargo ship carrying new rose bushes to the Empress.

In 1859 Edward FitzGerald privately published, through Bernard Quaritch, the first two hundred and fifty copies of his translation of the *Rubáiyat of Omar Khayyám*, in which the rose is often symbolically mentioned. These first copies went unsold at five shillings each and were eventually put in a discount box at a mere penny a piece. Legend has it that the great poet AC Swinburne bought a discounted copy and lent it, with his recommendation, to Dante Gabriel and Christina Georgina Rossetti, who also liked it and spread the word. Now, just over one hundred and fifty years later, it is one of the world's most known and best loved poems and, despite the fact that it has been translated many times by others, FitzGerald's paraphrase translation (in five editions), remains peerless. As for the first edition itself, only fifty copies are known to have survived and copies now change hands for magnificent sums. The Damask rose bush (*Rosa damascena mill.*), which was grown from a hip brought from a rosebush on the grave of Omar Khayyám in the gardens of Shadyakh, in the old city of Nishapur, Persia and planted, in 1893, at the head of FitzGerald's grave in Boulge churchyard, Suffolk is still there in a protective cage, as shown in Plate 23. To the right of the picture (at the foot of the grave), are more rose bushes, that were the gift of the government of Iran in 1972.

Now there are: old garden roses; modern garden roses (dating from the cultivar *La France* in 1867) and wild roses. There are different growing styles: standard roses (on one main stalk, including weeping standards), shrub roses, climbing roses, rambling roses, and miniature roses; there are heavily scented roses and roses in just about every colour, including darkest of dark crimson, near-black, but excepting green.

The scent of roses is known to most of us and I can distinctly recall pushing my infant face into the dewy heads of big, velvety, crimson rose blooms of the then fairly new Josephine Bruce, inhaling deeply and wondering at the marvellous scent of them. For long, people have cultivated roses for their appearance and their natural perfume as well as for their precious, essential oil, extracted as attar of roses and rose absolute, used in perfumery and rose water; their medicinal and their nutritional properties, to be found in their growing shoots, their petals and their hips, used to make rose syrup and rosehip syrup. 'A bed of roses' is a familiar expression as a description of being in a desirable state or situation and a 'rose-tinted' view of the world suggests an optimistic view of things. The Romans lay and dined under pergolas and in arbours of roses, when secrets might be disclosed in confidence and things said '*sub rosa*' are still treated as confidential. The remembered expression is the Latin for 'under the rose' but there is also evidence to suggest that the Greeks observed the same convention, deriving from Aphrodite's gift to Eros of a rose as a prompt to the reign of silence over the indiscretions of the gods. The ancients also floated rose petals in their wine and scattered rose petals on the floor at feasts; to maintain good humour and seemly behaviour and Cleopatra's palace was habitually carpeted with rose petals. Amongst others, the Indians scatter rose petals before a bride and over the marriage bed. In William Wyler's 1942 stirring wartime film, *Mrs Miniver*, starring Greer Garson in the title role, part of the storyline is the naming of a newly cultivated rose '*Mrs Miniver*', as a symbol of steadfastness. In fact there was then, in 1944, cultivated a large, cupped, fragrant, scarlet-crimson rose which was so named, although it seems difficult to find for sale.

Roses may adorn any occasion, from a joyful engagement to the wedding, on then to a birth; the Christening; birthdays; anniversaries, and, as symbols of the hope and joy of the resurrection, they even lighten grief and sorrow on the deathbed and at funerals. In short, of all flowers, roses are never, the world around, out of place, misunderstood or unwelcome.

Making a rose garden

Roses favour a warm, dry, sunny aspect, with soil of clay or loam, not chalk and a neutral to an acidic soil, which may be ensured by digging over the rose beds and mixing in good, rotted farmyard manure. Plant roses in the dormant season but never in frost and ensure that the roots are damp and not dried out. If necessary, immerse them in water overnight to soak them. Dig your holes so that they are big enough to spread the roots out and deep enough to cover the bottom of the growing point of the central stem(s). Mix some bone and blood meal into the earth at the bottom of the hole but mix it in well to avoid burning the roots. Place the rose plant and fill the hole; stamping the earth down fairly firmly and give a good watering in.

Old rose beds either need to be left to recover for two to three years before replanting or cleansed with Jeyes' Fluid or one of the proprietary cleansers on the market. The alternative is to replace the soil.

As for pruning: do this between February and March and perform this so that the cuts are at angle away from, and a little above, the nodes or buds that are to be kept on each stem. Prune new plantings quite hard the first year. Climbers you prune as you train them out by fanning and securing the stems to trellis (not too tightly and with plastic-coated wire), keeping the centre of the plant clear of too much growth. Ramblers need only light pruning. Repeat-flowering shrubs should be pruned in February to March and again when you remove the dead heads from the first flowering. Some people also prune roses lightly in November, after the flowering has finished.

As to choices of roses to plant: this is a personal thing and the best thing to do is to visit first rate nurseries, such as those at Peter Beales Roses or those of David Austin or of Trevor White. As already mentioned, there are old roses, new roses and something for everyone's choice and new hybrids are being produced all the time, such as *Grosvenor House* (a hybrid tea rose)and *Highgrove* (a modern climbing rose), from Peter Beales Roses, introduced at the Royal Chelsea Flower Show in 2009.

Roses under glass

If you wish to have roses the year round, in temperate climates, then you will need to bring some in under glass. Yearling, hybrid perpetual rose, tea rose and China rose bushes are the best for this. De-bud the chosen bushes in August and September then bring them inside an unheated greenhouse (preferably with a southerly aspect), in October and put them in six to eight inch terracotta pots containing a mixture of loam, well-rotted manure and a little sand to ease drainage because, although rose bushes can take good watering they should not be left standing in water. For February flowers, you will need to prune in November; on yearling plants leave two *eyes* (that is the beginning of the new growth) on each stem and leave two or three on each stem of older plants and keep growing shoots to a maximum of twelve on each bush. Once the buds begin to swell, start watering with liquid manure which should be prepared by putting a small sack of rotted manure in a bucket and soaking it in water to make a mixture about the shade of pale ale. Watering with this might be alternated with watering with soot water. During the summer months these plants should be put outside and de-budded as mentioned above.

It is also worth noting that some roses, such as tea roses, will root and grow from a slip of stem taken off with a 'heel' of bark and the best 'heels' are made by taking off, at the junction with the main stem, a branch from which a flower has been cut. Just place the heel in a jar of water in which (for cleanliness), you have mixed in a little charcoal. This is, though, a slow way to grow new rose bushes.

For further information and advice on roses and their cultivation, there is the Royal National Rose Society as well as some excellent books such as: the *RHS Encyclopaedia of Roses*.

Orchid growing

Owing to the enthusiasms of the great Victorian and Edwardian plant collectors and the great orchid collection (actually begun around 1780) of what became the Royal Horticultural Society, orchid collecting and culture became a craze for those who could afford it and people have even run high risks (sometimes of life and limb), to secure new and rare specimens from around the world. Some, such as former Prime Minister Neville Chamberlain's father, Joseph (an industrialist and politician), even had their own botanists to care for their collections.

There are over eight hundred and eighty genera of orchid; well over twenty thousand species and one hundred thousand hybrids. Orchids are beautiful, mysterious and erotic (flowers are, after all, the reproductive organs of plants and the word 'orchid' derives from the Greek for testicle; eighteenth century popular fancy even had it that they were sprung from the spilled semen of mating animals). Sweet or even foul-scented types may be found, as well as many different sizes, shapes and colours. The foulest-smelling orchid (it smells of rotting carrion), is said to be *bulbophyllum Phalaenopsis*; it is also one of the costliest to buy.

Examples of those genera often found in hothouse cultivation and on the market are: *Phalaenopsis* (the moth orchid); *Zygopetalum*; *Odontoglossum*: *Cymbidium*; *Paphiopedilum Phragmipedium*; *Cypripedium* (the lady's slipper orchid); *Ansellia*; *Cattleya* (which famously features in Marcel Proust's writings); *Dendrobium*; *Dendrochilum*; *Masdevallia*; and *Oncidium*.

Examples of hardier types that will even brave the English winter are *Dactylorhiza* and *Bletilla*.

A couple of good books to give you a deeper understanding, especially on housing, heating and cultivation are those mentioned in the bibliography; respectively, by William Cullina and Liz Johnson. Liz Johnson is also the owner of the award-winning orchid nursery McBean Orchids, at Lewes in East Sussex.

Bee-keeping

> Out of the strong came forth sweetness.
>
> Judges 14:14

There are several good reasons for keeping the honey bee (*Apis mellifera*) as an absorbing hobby: to pollinate flowers (especially in orchards) and to produce honey and wax and products from these substances, including the drink mead (from honey) and soaps, candles and polish (from wax). It is a little known fact that honey is a powerful antiseptic and has even been used as a contraceptive.

A colony of bees can sometimes produce as much as a hundred pounds (around forty-five kilograms) of honey a year. Honey is a sweet viscid material produced by bees, from flower nectar and contains dextrose, fructose, sucrose, maltose, vitamins, proteins and enzymes as well as tiny amounts of other substances, such as ash. There are seven grades of honey colour, from water white to dark amber. Besides honey and wax, bees also produce a sealant, called propolis, which they manufacture out of plant resins and use to seal gaps in the hive.

There is some evidence (from cave paintings in Spain), that bees have been actually domesticated for at least seven thousand years; although earliest man would have harvested honey from feral bees and, in some countries, wild honey is still harvested. In the UK now there are various local beekeepers' associations as well as the British Beekeepers' Association, founded in 1874. You really need to join one of the local groups to grasp the rudiments, including the lifecycles (egg, larva, pupa, adulthood) of each caste of bee: the queen; the drones and the workers, which make up each colony. The queen lays the eggs, after fertilization by the drones and the workers have various functions (some even lay eggs too) and, besides gathering nectar and foraging, some of them are nurses, guards and scouts.

Some people maintain that it is best for a novice to start off with a 'nucleus', that is to say a queen and six or seven combs, instead of a complete colony of ten or eleven combs and the queen. This will probably come to you as a 'boxed set' package, or artificial swarm, rather than a natural swarm. Bear in mind, though, that the queen can lay up to two thousand eggs a day so, before the summer is over, you are going to have a full colony and, probably, swarms looking for new lodgings. Obviously, at this point, you need to be prepared with fresh hives to take the new colonies and find the patience to coax them onboard.

There are several good books on the subject, such as that by Kim Flottum, mentioned in the bibliography. You will need to select the type of hives that suit you best and, of course, to find a suitable site. They say that bees like being near running water so setting them on a river or stream edge is a good place just make sure that your bees are not going to annoy your neighbours.

There are six main types of hives, including WBC ('William Broughton Carr') hives and then the most popular for hobby beekeeping, the 'national hives'. There is also an ultra-modern beehaus, produced by a firm called Omlet, which is designed specifically for beekeeping in small gardens or even on rooftops.

You are going to need to buy protective clothing and a hat and veil as well as a smoker to subdue the bees, when you are dealing with the hive; then there are feeders and a flat hive tool; it is also useful to have a small hammer in the kit. Generally, but especially when buying bees and hives, you must be aware that there are diseases and the worst of them is American or (as the case may be), European Foul Brood; both of which can strike in Europe. Therefore, always try to get under the wing of an expert apiarist when you are starting out. You must be aware that, come what may, you are going to suffer an occasional sting, no matter how careful you are, but this is a small price to pay for all the rewards of this fascinating and productive pastime.

Chicken keeping

A hen is only an egg's way of making another egg.

Samuel Butler

Domesticated chickens (*Gallus domesticus*) in many varieties and even sizes (such as diminutive bantam breeds), are all descended from the Asian red jungle fowl (*Gallus gallus*) and have been domesticated for around five thousand years.

French Maran hens and Copper Maran hens produce fabulously dark brown eggs, which, free range or barn-laid, are a delight to eat soft-boiled in their shells. One advantage that barn-laid eggs have over free range eggs is that, with true free range eggs, you can never be entirely sure how old the eggs are (as you find them in hedges and all over the place), whereas, with barn-laid eggs, you can be reasonably sure that the eggs are fresh. After all, there is little quite as nasty at breakfast as encountering a rotten egg; even if it is *good in parts*.

If you have enough land to keep some chickens then I suggest that you build a run out of fine-meshed chicken wire stapled on to wooden posts and that you dig it in for about a foot underground to keep the chickens in and vermin and predators out. Install a chicken coop, complete with nest boxes, that is adequate for the number of birds that you want to keep and ensure that they have a good supply of fresh water, suitable mixed grains and grit as well as a weekly allowance of greens, such as cabbage and kale, together with fresh straw from which to line their nests. Clearly, you need to muck-out the run and coop from time to time to prevent it fouling up. There are books on the subject of chicken-keeping, such as that mentioned by Chris Graham, in the bibliography.

Vegetables and salads

If you decide to keep honey bees and chickens, then you are bound to want to grow your own vegetables too; bearing in mind, of course, the usual descriptions, so that strawberries are counted as fruits (although they are really vegetables) and tomatoes are counted as vegetables (although they are really fruits).

Vegetables should be grown in crop rotation, comprising four-year cycles, so that the same vegetable is grown in the same plot only every few years. This lessens the likelihood of diseases taking hold.

For your vegetable patch, choose an open, sunny spot, near a water source with fertile, manured, deep, friable, well-drained topsoil. Dig this over, before planting to a depth of at least eight to ten inches. The rows of the same type of vegetable may be either eighteen inches apart or in beds four feet square; having small square beds avoids trampling the earth between rows. Unless you live in an especially warm part of your country, bring on seeds indoors, following the instructions on the packet and plant out only once the fear of frost has gone.

The main types of vegetables are (and some families or categories overlap):

Allium; this family includes: onions, garlic, shallots, leeks, asparagus and chives. Shallots make the superlative 'pickled onions': just skin them, top and tail them and put them in a jar with malt vinegar and pickling peppers. Seal it up and keep it shut up for six weeks or more and then enjoy with farmhouse cheese and a good farmhouse cider! *Asparagus officinalis* has been known and used for thousands of years as the Egyptians, Greeks and Romans cultivated it. It has diuretic properties. In Britain, it has a relatively short season from late April to mid-June and the Vale of Evesham in Worcestershire is famed for its production of this vegetable, which it celebrates with an annual week-long festival, during which the best of the crop is auctioned in around late May; The Fleece Inn featuring largely in the events. Some maintain that, although asparagus is available all year round from big producers in South America, Mexico and so on, English asparagus is the best. It likes a saline soil, which is tolerated by few other plants, and the time for planting out the crowns is the winter.

Brassicaceae; this is the mustard family and includes: cabbage, cauliflower, Brussels sprouts, broccoli, rocket.

Cucurbitaceae; this is the squash family and includes: cucumbers, pumpkins, melons and edible gourd squashes.

Fabaceae; this is the family of legumes, and includes: peas, beans, peanuts, lentils, chick peas.

Solanaceae; this is the nightshade family and (besides deadly nightshade), includes tomatoes, peppers, aubergines and potatoes.

Leafy Greens; these are lettuce, spinach, chard, collards, mustard, cress, rocket, chicory. I have to say that my favourites from the salad patch are Cos (or Romaine) lettuce (*Latuca sativa var. longifolia*), especially with cold roast beef and fresh horseradish sauce and rocket (of which there are many different types; salad rocket being *Eruca vesicaria ssp sativa*).

Root vegetables; these include: carrots, parsnips, potatoes, radishes, turnips, swedes, and sweet potatoes.

A good all round book on this subject, especially where space is limited, is that published by Dorling Kindersley, mentioned in the Bibliography.

Fruit

Orchard fruits

These principally include: apples, pears, quince, cherries, plums and figs. In some warmer places, peaches, nectarines and apricots may also be grown.

Apples (*Malus domestica*) were introduced to Britain by the Romans and early types include Old English dessert apples and Costard cooking apples (from which we get the word 'costermonger'). By the Victorian age there were developed over two thousand varieties of dessert apples as well as those for culinary use and cider. The National Fruit Collection in Kent has the biggest collection of apple varieties in the world and the UK is the only country to produce apples, such as Bramley's and Cox's, specifically for cooking. Nowadays, Cox's Orange Pippin accounts for most UK dessert apple production but Braeburn and Egremont Russets are also popular.

Pears (*Pyrus*) seem to have been cultivated in Britain before the Roman occupation. There are around three thousand varieties, including Bartlett, Comice, Concorde, Wardon and then the perry pears such as Arlingham Squash, Parsonage, Yoking House and those with the fantastic names that I mention in *Men About Town*, in relation to perry-making.

Quince (*Cydonia oblonga*) Remember *The Owl and the Pussycat*, by Edward Lear:

> *They dined on mince and slices of quince*
> *Which they ate with a runcible spoon;*
> *And hand in hand, on the edge of the sand,*
> *They danced by the light of the moon,*
> *The moon,*
> *The moon,*
> *They danced by the light of the moon.*

Quince cannot be eaten raw and needs to be cooked and turned into jam or jelly, in which form it can indeed be sliced, to be edible.

Cherries (*Prunus*) Here there are several good varieties : Bradbourne Black ; Early Rivers; Frogmore Early (cultivated by Thomas Ingram at Frogmore, Windsor in 1864); Napoleon and, for cherry tart there are Montmorency and Morello.

Plums (*Prunus*) Closely related to cherries, these also include damsons and green gages. The oldest plum in cultivation is probably *Prunus salicina*, taken to Japan from China. The Greeks brought plums from Syria and the Romans brought them to northern Europe. They have been cultivated in England for centuries and the famous and popular *Victoria* plum was first cultivated in Sussex in the 1840s.

Mulberry (*Morus*) There are black, red and white varieties, judged according to the colour of the ripened fruit which, although delicious, sadly is often left to rot, as few people actually know what it is. The leaves are famously fed to silkworm (hence their scientific name of *Bombyx mori*) and, of course there is the nursery rhyme:

> *Here we go round the mulberry bush,*
> *The mulberry bush,*
> *The mulberry bush.*
> *Here we go round the mulberry bush,*
> *On a cold and frosty morning.*

There is a magnificent example of a mature mulberry tree just outside Lincoln's Inn Library in central London.

The reason we have so many mulberry trees in England is that James I sought to establish a native silk industry. However, most of the trees planted were black mulberries (*morus nigra*), and the fussy silkworm will eat only the leaves of the white mulberry (*morus alba*). Fortunately, the mulberry in Lincoln's Inn is the black variant: otherwise it would have long died.

Figs (*Ficus carica*) This is a fruit eaten since prehistoric times and by many ancient people, as well as being from the tree which (according to Genesis 3:7), gave Adam and Eve cover on their expulsion from the Garden of Eden:

> *Then the eyes of them both were opened, and they knew that they were naked; and they sewed fig leaves together, and made themselves aprons.*

The fig is indigenous to Asia and the Mediterranean but it also grows in warmer parts of the UK, especially favouring a south or south-west facing wall. Ideally you should pick them when they are sun-warmed and fully ripe (dark green or brown tinged with a reddish colour) and consume immediately as they do not keep long. This fruit is rich in nutrients and minerals and contains anti-oxidants, as well as having a laxative effect. I once saw them for sale on a barrow in Kingsway, London, under the banner *A Run for Your Money*!

The book by the Harry Barker and the RHS in the Bibliography is a good general guide, as it is for the next section too.

Soft and bush fruits

Strawberries: incomparably the best-tasting are alpine strawberries (*Flagaria vesca*). There are several good varieties, including *Baron Solemacher*, *Mara des Bois* and *Gariguette*. They need well-drained soil, rich in humus. Dig this over and manure it well. Plant out your seedlings or plants in the Spring, after the last frost and water-in well. Spreading barley straw around between the plants protects the fruit from water damage but, in any event, harvest and eat the berries as soon as ripe. Moreover, for a change, instead of sugar and cream, try grinding some black pepper over them.

Raspberries: probably, my favourite fruit of all and it is certainly one of the first that I remember in my grandparents' gardens. Most cultivars derive from hybrids of *Rubus idaeus* and *Rubus strigosus* and there are varieties which all fruit at different times through the summer and autumn. They are sometimes thought to have originated in Asia but, certainly, the Romans knew them. The British improved the strains.

Loganberries: this is an accidental hybrid between a blackberry (probably *Rubus vitifolius*) and a raspberry (probably *Rubus idaeus*) by an American called

James Harvey Logan in the late 1880s, when he was trying to hybridise blackberries to find an improved cultivar. These fruits are especially good in traditional sherry trifle and in jams.

Gooseberries: these are native to Europe and Western Asia. In the sixteenth century, they were cultivated in Britain for their supposed medicinal qualities. It was not long before the merits of gooseberry pie, crumble and fool were discovered and many varieties were developed in the nineteenth century. In 1905 there was a plague of mildew and most of the bushes were wiped out; being replaced by American hybrids and the main cultivated species now is *Ribes grossularia*. The plants should be planted out in the autumn in well-manured soil in a sunny but sheltered spot and dead wood should be pruned off in the winter. If you are interested in competing in a show with your gooseberry produce, Egerton Bridge Old Gooseberry Society (established in 1801, in Yorkshire) holds an annual contest on the first Tuesday in August.

Rhubarb: (*Rheum x hybridium*) Varieties of rhubarb have been cultivated in China for thousands of years and its popularity has gradually spread around the world. Strictly speaking, it is a vegetable but, of course, is used as a fruit in pies and crumble-pudding dishes, when it is best served with egg custard.

Blackberries: (*Rubus fruticosus*) is not a berry at all but a bramble fruit that grows widely in the northern hemisphere. Blackberry picking in late summer and early Autumn is a delightful way to spend a lazy afternoon, as these fruits can be made into jam or combined with apples in blackberry and apple pie. However, owing to their vigorous growth and amazing root systems, they can soon take over a garden and so their cultivation in the garden is not especially recommended.

Black currants; red currants: and these (*Ribes rubrum*; *Ribes nigrum*) are not really currants but berries! They are native to much of the northern hemisphere and the so-called 'white currant' is a variant (or 'sport') of the red currant. All are widely used in cooking and black currant jam is widely available and popular, as is red currant jelly. They are plentiful sources of vitamins B and C; black currants are also made into cordials and syrups, such as *Ribena*; which is right up there with *Marmite* and *Bovril* as British peculiarities. If you grow these fruits they need shade as direct sun can easily scorch their leaves.

Dessert grapes: (*Vitis vinifera*) grapes are fruits that have grown since pre-historic times. They are first known for certain to have been eaten around

5000 BC in Asia and Iran. Grapes (as '*the fruit of the vine*') are referred to in the Bible; maybe most famously, at the Last Supper, as recorded in Matthew 26:29:

> *But I say unto you, I will not drink henceforth of the fruit of the vine, until that day when I drink it new with you in my Father's kingdom.*

Grapes have been cultivated since around 3200BC in the Near East. The Egyptians also had grapes and the Greeks and Romans were largely responsible for introducing them to Europe and for the viticulture which has now spread all around the New World, with considerable success. Grapes generally like a neutral soil and, unless you are aiming at commercial production (when you would grow them laterally in rows), it is probably best to train them over a trellis or pergola. Plant new vines in the winter or early spring and keep them well watered. Remove all fruit until the third year and then remove the smallest two bunches on each spur and even remove the smallest grapes on each bunch. Prune when the vines are dormant in the winter by reducing the leading rods by half their length and take the lateral shoots off the rods back to one bud. A good white variety is *Siegerrebe* and another is *Madeleine Angevine*. Good black types are *Brant* and *Queen of Esther*.

Nuts

Almonds: (*Prunis dulcis*) The Common Almond will grow and even fruit in southern parts of the UK but these trees need protection from the frost and a warm, southerly aspect in which to thrive.

Cobnuts: So far as British production is concerned the cobnut or the filbert is the most widespread cultivated nut. It derives from the wild hazelnut (*Corylus avellana*) and has been cultivated in England (especially the Home Counties), since the sixteenth century in nut groves, called *plats*. The variety called the Kentish Cob is the favourite and this dates from around 1830. The Kentish Cobnuts Association is a club for growers and arranges showings of produce at the National Fruit Show (nationalfruitshow.org.uk) and stages an *Annual Nutters' Supper* and, as a matter of fact, I do actually know a couple of these Nutters . Without going so far as entering commercial production, and not least for the right to attend the supper, one could always find room for a nut tree or two within the orchard. The trees in the plats also used to be coppiced, to produce rods of hazel-wood for basket-making.

Pine nuts: Good examples of suitable varieties are *Pinus armandii* and *Pinus pinea* and the nuts harvested from their cones are delicious in salads; especially mixed into a Waldorf salad and, of course, they feature in the best type of pesto sauce.

Sweet chestnuts: (*Castanea sativa*) will grow in the UK but fruit only in the south of the country and most successfully of all in the south-east. There are some splendid examples in Greenwich Park, South East London. Of course, the fruits are best eaten roasted over hot coals (or even in an oven) but, either way, do remember to prick them or you will have multiple explosions on your hands. The *Maron de Lyon* variety is especially recommended.

Walnuts: Of these, for nuts, the Persian Walnut (*Julgans regia*) grows best in the UK and the varieties Buccanneer and Broadview are especially good as they fruit after only two years. You can pick and pickle the immature fruit in July or wait until the full harvest in October. As already noted, seasoned walnut wood is especially prized for gun stocks (as well as ornamental woodwork, such as dashboard fascias).

Hothouse fruits

Citrus fruits are the most obvious, followed by bananas but you will need a tall hothouse for bananas and, frankly, you are never going to recoup the cost, so if you wish to have hothouse fruit, you are probably best to confine your attention to citrus fruits, melons and, possibly, pineapples and kiwi fruits. The traditional way of growing melons in Britain was to make melon pits inside low concrete walls, fill this with rotting manure and put a removable roof of glass (sloping from back to front at fifteen degrees) on the top. The heat from the rotting manure brings the fruit on. Obviously, you face the pit into the sun. For more on this and gardening generally, see the book mentioned in the Bibliography by J C Loudon. There is a kiwi fruit plant growing on a sheltered outside wall of the Italian garden in the *Gardens of Heligan*, in central Cornwall.

Collecting wild mushrooms and fungi

The fine detail of this is outside the scope of this book and absolutely certain knowledge of what you are harvesting is necessary as there are poisonous fungi which can be mistaken for edible fungi and consumption of some of them (such as the False Chanterelle (*Hygrophoropsis aurantiaca*), can result in serious poisoning, and some, such as *Cortinarius rubellus*, and the very common Panther Cap (*amanita*

101

pantherina) and Death Cap (*amanita phalloides*) can and frequently do cause death. However, I mention the topic as, once you know what you are doing (confining yourself to the readily identifiable edible fungi), mushroom picking is a most satisfying autumnal occupation. Roger Phillips' book *Mushrooms* has been hailed as a masterpiece for those seeking a plain guide to clear identification.

Essential specifications for wine cellars big and small; construction, temperature and humidity

> Wer nicht liebt Wein, Weib und Gesang,
> Der bleibt ein Narr sein Leben lang.
>
> Martin Luther

The essential specifications for a wine 'cellar' are that you need a space which, whether with assistance or not, maintains a constant ambient temperature of 11–12°C (avoiding fluctuations); you want a relative humidity of sixty per cent (to stop corks drying out) and it is also best to avoid vibration and direct sunlight. There are fairly simple devices that can be purchased to regulate temperature and humidity and the companies mentioned below will be able to advise on these.

There are various other options.

First, there is the option of storing your wine in optimum conditions with the vintner until you need it but this is not always convenient if you need wine in a hurry and, moreover, there are storage and delivery charges imposed. Secondly, there is the wine cabinet, configured rather like a refrigerator but, obviously with strict limitations on volume. Makers include: Liebehrr, Miele, Vintec and The Corner Fridge Company.

Larger cabinets are made by Eurocave, Traustherm and, again The Corner Fridge Company. Vinosafe go so far as to provide a self-assembly wine cellar but you obviously need a cellar in the first place. Then there are also 'spiral cellars' that are set into the ground and supplied and fitted by Spiral Cellars Ltd.

There is a great book on this subject, by Richard M Gold, and it is listed under his name in the Bibliography.

Just a side-note on this subject of wine: when you are out drinking wine, the sommelier will often offer you the cork, the idea is that sniffing it will tell you (as it has already told him) that the wine is not 'corked' (i.e. gone off by oxidation, caused by exposure to air in the bottle). Subject to your direction, he will also pour some in your glass for you to test. Again, the purpose of this is only to enable you to assure yourself that the wine is not corked and you can determine this by gently swirling the wine in the glass and smelling it. Corked wine smells mouldy or of vinegar (which, in fact, it has become). You need to get some corked wine and give it a good sniffing to understand and recall the smell. It also often has a cloudy appearance. There is no need to taste the wine poured into your glass at this stage. However, if you do, there is no point in expressing a view on whether you like it or not: you have, after all, decided this when you ordered it. Of course, you can accept the cork when offered, make your decision on that (backed by the sommelier's judgement), and then, assuming that the wine is not corked, signal to the sommelier to proceed to pour it to drink, in the usual way, for your guest(s) and for you.

If you happen to be pouring your own wine, remember the saying;

'Girl by the waist; bottle by the neck.'

That said, an exception might be a champagne bottle because a demonstration has suggested to me that holding a champagne bottle with the thumb in the punt (indentation in the base), with fingers extended out along the length of the bottle, really does inhibit the wine from bubbling over when it is poured gently into a glass held at a slant but this has since been explained to me as wholly to do with the slant of the glass.

Most glasses are best held by the top of the stem; this is best for controlling it when swirling the wine and there used to be a point observed of not holding objects with the fingertips; especially when passing them to someone else. However, for anything properly served in a brandy balloon, cradle the glass in your hand to warm it: the same goes for a glass of wine that has been served over-chilled.

CHAPTER 8

National and International Social and Sporting Events

No man can have society upon his own terms. If he seeks it, he must serve it too.

Ralph Waldo Emerson

I do not pretend that this list is anywhere near exhaustive but I hope that it presents a reasonable selection of events across a range of activities. I give a short description of what used to be the London Season and its most important events at the beginning of Chapter 8 of *History of Men's Fashion*. The events that have survived the official demise of the Season itself, have done so because they are worthwhile in themselves and not just part of an air-headed social whirl.

JANUARY

Vienna Philharmonic New Year's Day Concert

This has taken place in the Grosser Saal of the Musikverein in Vienna each New Year's Day since 1939 (although the first concert actually took place on 31st December 1938). Some of us will remember fondly the days when the orchestra was conducted by Willi Boskowsky but, nowadays, there are guest conductors. The music played celebrates the works of the Strauss family and their contemporaries. It is so popular that registration for tickets takes place a year before each concert and the concert itself is broadcast all around the world. It is one of those events at which members of the *audience* still actually go to some trouble and dress in morning dress.

London International Boat Show

This takes place in early to mid-January in London's Docklands.

Australian (Tennis) Open

This takes place from mid to late January, at Melbourne Park.

Monte Carlo Rally

This takes place around 22 to 25 January and has been organized by the Auto Club de Monaco since 1911. It is followed by the **Historic Rally** for which only cars that were built between 1955–1988 are eligible.

Burns' Night

25 January is Burns' Night when the Scots (wherever they may be in the world) congregate to celebrate, with a Burns' Supper, the birthday of the great Scotch poet Robbie Burns (1759–1796); author of some poems that are read and loved wherever the Scots-English language is spoken; including: *Tam O'Shanter; Address to a Haggis; Auld Lang Syne* and *My Love is Like a Red, Red Rose.*

At the more formal suppers, the full order of proceedings is as follows: there are words of welcome from the host and then the *Selkirk Grace* is said:

> *Some hae meat and canna eat,*
> *And some wad eat that want it,*
> *But we hae meat and we can eat,*
> *And sae the Lord be thankit.*

All then remain standing to receive the haggis (comprising sheep offal, onion, oats etc., cooked in a sheep's stomach), served with mashed neeps (turnips or swede) and tatties (potatoes), as the chef is piped and slow hand-clapped with it to the top table. The host or another diner then recites the *Address to A Haggis* and, at the line *'an cut you up wi' ready slight'* he or she, with gusto, cuts the haggis open, to applause and a toast to the Haggis in whisky; after which there follows the meal and then the Loyal Toast and any other toasts. After this there is a speech To the Immortal Memory of Robbie Burns; The Toast to the Lassies and a response from a Lassie and then, of course, more poems and songs. The evening ends with much carousing; everyone singing *Auld Lang Syne* and then taking great care not to trip over their snow shoes on their way *hame.*

FEBRUARY

Six Nations' Championship

This is a lengthy rugby tournament staged between England, Scotland, Ireland, Wales, France and Italy and it begins in February. The Calcutta Cup (dating from 1872), is awarded to the winner of the England v Scotland match.

MARCH

Berkeley (Summer) Dress Show

This is now an early, fund-raising event held at various times and in various locations each year in which wannabee 'debutantes', who get through an application process, strut their stuff on the catwalk.

Vienna State Opera Ball

This takes place in early March and is one of the few regular white tie affairs left in the world. The Vienna Court Opera House (as it was known before 1920), opened with a performance of Mozart's Don Giovanni on 25 May 1869. The opera house was rebuilt after the Second World War and re-opened with a performance of Beethoven's *Fidelio* in 1955.

Rio de Janeiro Carnaval

Note the local spelling as most people get it wrong. The word derives from the Latin for 'farewell meat' and is a moveable festival preceding the forty days of Lenten Fast. This has to be the biggest street party in the world; its highlight is the samba dancers who, *shakin' it*, strut their feathered and spangled stuff in the Sambodromo in the centre of the Marvellous City.

Cheltenham Festival

This famous racing festival is for three days in mid-March and includes the coveted Cheltenham Gold Cup. The Lincoln Handicap takes place towards the end of the month. The first local proper course was on the West Down of Cleeve Hill (with a grandstand) for a meeting in 1819, which was a three-day event of flat racing. The main race was for the Cheltenham Gold Cup on the third day. The 1819 race was won by Spectre. A meeting held in 1829 was disrupted by a congregation led by The Reverend Francis Close, a local Hellfire and Brimstone Anglican clergyman and he even went on to orchestrate an arson attack which burned down the grandstand! Racing moved to Prestbury Park between 1831 and 1834; in 1835 it returned to Cleeve Hill but the flat race meetings fell into decline. In 1834 at Andoversford was held the first Grand Annual Steeplechase, which is the oldest race in the jump racing calendar. This event was moved to Prestbury Park but the land was sold in 1853 and racing ceased. In 1881, Prestbury Park was sold on to W A Baring Bingham who restarted jump racing there in 1898 and there it has remained. Between 9 and 10 April 1902 Prestbury Park hosted its first National Hunt Festival, which included the National Hunt Chase (a race first run in 1860). This race settled at Prestbury Park in 1911, for which a new stand was built. The Festival was extended to three days in 1923 and in 1924 there was introduced a three mile steeple chase for which the prize was, once again, the Cheltenham Gold Cup (won, in that year, by Red Splash). In1927 a Champion Hurdle race was also introduced. Golden Miller won the Cheltenham Gold Cup on five consecutive occasions between 1932 and 1936 and even won both the Gold Cup and the Grand National in 1934 (a feat that has never been equalled by any horse in the same season). Arkle, won three consecutive Gold Cups between 1964 and 1966 and there is a commemorative statue of him at the course. There is a big Irish presence at Cheltenham, very much in evidence on St Patrick's Day 2006, when the first three places in the Gold Cup were taken by Irish horses. The Cheltenham Gold Cup is fashioned anew every year.

Oxford-Cambridge University Boat Race

This takes place annually, between two rowing eights and a cox from each of the University boat clubs, on the last Saturday in March or the first Saturday in April, on a course which is four miles and three hundred and seventy-four yards long, upstream on the River Thames, between Putney and Mortlake. The first such race took place in 1829 but it has (except for wartime) taken place every year since 1856. The north (Middlesex) and the south (Surrey) sides of the river are called 'stations', and a coin is tossed by the umpire to decide who will choose the station to be taken by each side. There has been one dead heat (in 1877) and both boats sank in 1912. The banks of the river are crowded with thousands of spectators for each year's event, which is also broadcast around the world.

APRIL

US (Golf) Masters

This takes place at the beginning of April at Augusta National Golf Club, in Georgia and is by invitation only. The winner is awarded the famous 'green jacket'.

Grand National

One of the world's most famous horse races, run at Aintree, in early April. The current course is two-and-a-quarter miles and has sixteen fences. The horses go round nearly twice and jump thirty fences in all before the four hundred and ninety-four yard home straight. The first official race was in 1839; although racing at Aintree had first been organized by William Lynn of the Waterloo Hotel in 1829, when he leased land at Aintree and built a grandstand. The 1836 race was won by The Duke, ridden by Captain Becher (after whom was later named the difficult fence 'Becher's Brook'); the first official race in 1839 was won by Lottery. In 1847 the race was named the 'Grand National Handicap Steeplechase'. The first horse to win in two consecutive years was Abd-El-Kader in 1850 and 1851 and the horse to win by the biggest margin was Cloister, by forty lengths, in 1893. Red Rum's feat of three Grand National wins (in 1973, 1974 and 1977) is the stuff of legend as was Bob Champion's win on the previously crocked Aldaniti in 1981 (Champion himself having just recovered from cancer).

The Ancient Game of Hurling

The principal annual game of hurling takes place on Shrove Tuesday which, of course, depends on when Easter falls. The event that I am most familiar with is the St Columb hurling in central Cornwall, which happens to be my mother's home town, and I recall that my grandparents had in their possession a very old and pitted hurling ball. Another one, held in the family, is illustrated in Plate 20. Long ago, the game (which has nearly no rules and no referee), used to be played all over Cornwall but now is confined to St Columb and St Ives and is probably as ancient as the *Obby Oss* at Padstow and the *Furry Dance* at Helston. It is a rough and tumble game that has been played since pre-Norman times, with a ball, about the size of a cricket ball, covered in beaten silver with a raised silver seam on which a motto traditionally appears. This used to be in the ancient Cornish language but one of the modern versions of this is '*Town and Country Do Your Best*', which is a reference to the fact that the game is played between teams of townsmen and countrymen whose objective is to run with and pass the ball to get it into the correct goal, the goals being placed two miles apart. The only taboo is to hide the ball, except in jest. The game begins in the market place at 4.30 pm, when the ball is 'called-up' by last year's winner, who holds it aloft and encourages his team to recapture it. In fact, the winner each year may keep the actual ball, provided that he replaces it, with one of local manufacture. He then 'throws-up' the ball from a stepladder, after calling out: '*Town and Country do your best for in this parish I must rest*' and raising three cheers. All hell then breaks loose in a giant scrummage of St Columbians of all ages; to the extent that shopkeepers and householders even board up their windows. The game can take many hours. The race over, the winner of the ball is then carried back to the market place, to the *Hurling Song*, where he proclaims whether the ball is won for Town or Country. Later on, everyone returns to the market place and the ball is 'called-up' again and a pub crawl takes place. The ball is repeatedly immersed in gallon flasks of beer (making it into 'silver beer') and this is shared around. Fortunately, despite the loss of so much custom and tradition, across the board, this game appears so deeply embedded in the local consciousness that it is likely to continue and I have even seen a photograph of a cousin of mine at a recent hurling.

Badminton Horse Trials

This is three days (around Eastertide), of dressage, cross country and show jumping events held in the park of Badminton House, the seat of the Duke of Beaufort, and has been held most years since 1948.

Sandown Park Gold Cup

Held at Esher in late April, this is the last of the season's jump racing.

Oban Ball

This is more fully described, under the heading 'Balls', below.

Padstow Obby Oss (Hobby Horse)

This is a pagan festival, maybe with overtones of fertility rites, that is celebrated on 1 May each year (or, if 1 May is a Sunday, on 2 May). Padstovians dress in white and, according to family tradition or mere whim, follow one of two 'Obby Osses' which are men dressed up and masked as hobby horses: one red and one blue. As they dance through the town and around the harbour, the Osses are 'teased' by female 'teasers'. There is also dancing around the Maypole in Broad Street. The whole thing makes an intriguing and enjoyable spectacle. As with all such festivities, there are all the customary refreshments.

Mille Miglia

This is a road race that, since 1927, has taken place in early May between Brescia (in commemoration of the early home of the Italian automotive industry) and Rome. The cars are *Gran Turismo* cars built between 1927 and 1955.

Helston Furry Dance

The Helston Furry Dance is an ancient celebration of Spring, pre-dating the Christian era but it takes place on 8 May each year, which happens to be the anniversary of the Apparition of St Michael (the town's patron saint), except when that is a Sunday or Monday (market day) and then it takes place on the preceding Saturday. Therefore, we may be fairly sure that it is a pagan festival that has been grafted onto a Christian tradition. One legend holds that it all began when a meteorite (*The Fiery Dragon*) fell into Angel Yard, Helston and the inhabitants of the town danced to celebrate their being spared destruction.

The celebration begins at dawn with the youths and maids of the town going out and collecting flowers and boughs to 'bring in the May' as well as lily of the valley for buttonholes. Garlands of flowers are hung around the town and the church bells 'ring in the day' at 6.30 am; there is dancing from 7 am. At 8.30 am there is the *Hal-an-Tow*, which is a mummers' play in which St George slays the dragon and St Michael slays the devil. The labyrinthine, organized dances include the children's dance, which takes place at 10 am, through the main street and in and out of shops and houses. The principal dance starts at noon by the town clock, outside the Corn Exchange, and is led off by the local grandees in full morning dress; the men wear lily of the valley buttonholes upright and the ladies wear the blooms inverted in *corsages* and only Helstonians may wear these flowers in the dance. The town band plays the famous tune of the ballad *The Flora Dance* (an alternative name). There is a final dance at 5 pm and then (as throughout), it is rounded off with *customary refreshments*. As well as '*Furry*' and '*Flora*', it has also been called the '*Faddy Dance*'. Finally, '*Furry*' is pronounced to rhyme with 'hurry'.

The FA Cup Final

This, in mid-May, is the last and the most important event in the English football calendar. Football, or soccer, is yet another game that England has given the world. Anciently, and brutally, played; it might have its origins in hurling, already mentioned. Cambridge University students, in the 1840s, tried to unify the rules (such as they were), which then varied from place to place. On 26 October 1863, the Football Association (the 'FA') was formed when twelve clubs and schools met in the Freemasons Tavern in central London and decided upon unified rules. Blackheath walked out because they refused to accept the proscription of 'hacking'. Under Ebenezer Cobb Morley, fourteen basic laws were established. The International FA Board, between the countries in the UK, was established on 2 June 1886 and decided that a three quarters' majority of votes was required to change the laws; a rule that still stands. Meanwhile, a Challenge Cup competition had been founded in 1871 and this became the FA Cup. Between 1923 and 2000, the final was played at Wembley Empire Stadium. While that was being rebuilt, the finals were played at the Millenium Stadium in Cardiff. It is now back at Wembley. The first international match was played between England and Scotland in 1872 and the first European internationals took place when England toured Europe in 1908. The FA rejoined FIFA after the Second World War and first took part in the World Cup in Brazil in 1950. Sadly, of late, the English representation in important international competitions has become a disappointing affair; reaching its nadir in the last World Cup competition. Let's hope that they can sharpen-up their act for next time. Meanwhile, there's always 1966…

Cricket at Lord's

There is evidence, from Court records relating to a land dispute, that cricket was played in England in the sixteenth century. It was probably played much earlier as a bat and ball game. There is also an ancient Indian game, still played, called *Gulle Danda* (Punjabi for 'ball' and 'stick'), from which the modern game may also, in part, derive. The old French *criquet* means 'club' and is the origin of the name for croquet which may be related to cricket.

The MCC: The Marylebone Cricket Club – is based at Lord's Cricket Ground at St John's Wood, North West London. The club was founded by Thomas Lord in 1787 on the site of what is now Dorset Square, London NW1. The first match took place between Middlesex and Essex on 31 May 1787. From this time, the club regulated the Laws of Cricket – beginning with prescription of the 22-yard pitch and how batsmen were to be given 'out' – howza!! rather than waza?? The club moved to the present ground in 1814; the Eton against Harrow match was begun, mainly to entertain the boys' fathers, in 1805. The Laws of cricket are now the responsibility of the England and Wales Cricket Board. 'The Ashes' series of matches between England and Australia dates from England's first loss to Australia on home ground (at the Oval) on 29 August 1882. The next day *The Sporting Times* ran a mock Obituary of English cricket and when the England team next went to Australia they vowed to return with the 'Ashes of the corpse'. The following Australian summer, the Ashes came to be represented by a small terracotta urn presented to England by Australia, after the England captain, Ivo Bligh, said that he had 'come to retrieve the ashes of English cricket.' The urn contains the ashes of either the bails or the ball used in a match at Rupertwood. The urn bears the poem:

> *When Ivo goes back with the urn, the urn;*
> *Studds, Steel, Read and Tylecote return, return;*
> *The welkin will ring loud,*
> *The great crowd will feel proud,*
> *Seeing Barlow and Bates with the urn, the urn;*
> *And the rest coming home with the urn.*

The original urn is now housed at the MCC clubhouse, while the trophy now officially representing the Ashes is a larger crystal urn. The Obituary ran:

An Affectionate Remembrance
Of
ENGLISH CRICKET
Which died at the Oval
on
29th August 1882
Deeply lamented by a large circle of sorrowing friends and acquaintances
RIP
NB – The body will be cremated and the ashes taken to Australia.

Punch magazine had also run a poem:

Well done, Cornstalks, whipt us
Fair and square
Was it luck that tripped us?
Was it scare?
Kangaroo land's 'Demon' or our own,
Want of devil, coolness, nerve, backbone?

The Australian Sir Donald George ('The Don') Bradman (1908–2001) is widely held to be the greatest batsman of all time and one of the greatest sportsmen of recorded history: aloof and restrained, he is a far cry from some of the sportsmen of today.

Correct dress for spectating cricket at Lord's is mentioned in Chapter 11 of *History of Men's Fashion*. Apart from that, for humble village club matches, the outfit suggested for Wimbledon should suffice.

One other point on sporting dress is this: Fred Astaire sometimes wore a scarf around his waistband and is often accredited with having introduced this jaunty touch.

However, the cartoon in Plate 21 puts paid to that idea: it is an 1889 *Spy* cartoon of Hylton '*Punch*' Philipson (1866–1935), a renowned sportsman of the time, wearing his Oxford 'Blue' as a scarf around his waist. University, school and club 'colours', especially 'Blues' and their equivalents (London University awards 'Purples') as awards for sporting prowess were once much more sported on the field than they are now and would often be worn as Philipson is wearing his.

Part of the reason for the current absence of 'colours' from the sporting field is that sport (or at least the sport that is broadcast to us), has largely ceased to be played for the honour of representing an institution or country and for the love of the game and has become Big Business, so that we are forced to watch professional players wearing, as advertisements, the logos of the corporations to whom they have sold their souls.

Maybe, Fred Astaire, because his sister (Adele) married a younger son of a Duke of Devonshire, picked up on the old English habit, of wearing ties and scarves as colours in this way, and just gave it an American twist!

Royal Windsor Horse Show

This takes place in mid-May and includes all the usual equestrian events, as well as carriage driving, which is the favourite activity of the Duke of Edinburgh.

Cannes Film Festival

This has been taking place for sixty years and the biggest prize is the Palme d'Or.

The PGA Championship

This golfing tournament takes place at Wentworth West Course in May. It had rotated between various courses but since 1984 it has been firmly planted at Wentworth.

Glyndebourne

The Glyndebourne Opera House opens in late May and the season goes on to the end of August. The opera at Glyndebourne was begun by the hereditary owner of the house, John Christie, who built an organ room and held amateur concerts there in the 1920s. To improve the quality of the entertainment, he engaged a professional opera singer (Audrey Mildmay), whom he subsequently married. They decided to do something on a grander scale while they were touring opera houses of Europe on their honeymoon. They built an opera house large enough to present Mozart's intimate operas. It opened on 28 May 1934 with a performance of *Le Nozze di Figaro*. The opera house was enlarged several times until it was replaced by an entirely new building (paid for largely by donation). This opened sixty years to the day after the first ever performance and the first performance in the new house was – again – *Le Nozze di Figaro*. The dress for this is normally black tie and dinner jacket.

The Royal Horticultural Show (The Chelsea Flower Show)

The Royal Horticultural Society was founded as the Horticultural Society in London in 1804, by Sir Joseph Banks and John Wedgwood, to promote improvements in horticulture and held the first shows in the 1820s. The 1850s were a low point in the Society's history, owing to lack of funding but, in 1861, Prince Albert, its President, arranged the granting of a Royal Charter and it even began to rebuild its depleted library in 1866, on the foundation of the library of John Lindley. 1903 saw the purchase of the famous garden at Wisley in Surrey, to which have been added the gifts of other gardens: Rosemoor, in Devon, and Hyde Hall, in Essex and it also runs Harlow Carr, in North Yorkshire. Since 1904 it has had an exhibition hall (where year round exhibitions are staged) and offices in Vincent Square, Victoria and these were expanded in 1928. From 1888, the big annual Spring show was held in the ancient Temple Gardens, off Fleet Street, until it moved to the Royal Hospital Gardens at Chelsea in 1913. The main annual show is normally for five days towards the end of May and it is as well to book well in advance.

Queen's Cup

This is played for at the Guards' Polo Club at Windsor between May and June. This is also the period during which is played the **French (Tennis) Open**.

Cheese-rolling and Wake

This has taken place for over two hundred years, on Coopers Hill, Brockworth, Gloucestershire. The modern event occurs on Spring Bank Holiday (at the end of May). A full double Gloucester cheese is rolled down the hill and the participants chase after it, the first to catch the cheese or, if no one catches it, the first over the finishing line, wins the cheese. By 2010, of course, although a rolling did take place, it had no official sponsorship, owing to the ubiquitous concerns over 'health and safety', which have even extinguished the fun of playing conkers in schools.

JUNE

Royal Bath and West Show

This agricultural show takes place, over four days, on a site which is twenty miles outside Bath, at the beginning of June.

London to Brighton Classic Car Run

This is a different event from the Veteran Car Run (which takes place in November), and is for pre-1985 classic cars and follows a different scenic route each year. Recently, the legendary Sir Stirling Moss has been flagging off participants.

Epsom Derby

This takes place on the Friday and Saturday at the beginning of June. The Friday is Ladies' Day and the Saturday is Derby Day. The event was begun by the then Earl of Derby in 1783 who organized with his friends a one mile race for their three year old fillies; since 1784 it has been one and a half miles. Morning dress is not essential but those who do make the effort should wear black silk toppers rather than Ascot greys.

Prix du Jockey Club

This has taken place at Chantilly, Oise, since 1836 and three-year-olds are raced over a testing course of a mile and a half.

Royal Cornwall Show

This agricultural show takes place over three days in early June and includes a steam exhibition.

Le Mans

The famous twenty-four hour race has taken place since 1923, over road and dedicated track, at Sarthe in France.

Trooping the Colour

> Some talk of Alexander,
> And some of Hercules
> Of Hector and Lysander,
> And such great men as these
> But of all the world's great heroes,
> There's none that can compare
> With the tow row, row, row, row, row, row
> Of the British Grenadier.

> From an old song, of uncertain origin

The Trooping the Colour ceremony has taken place, since 1748, in celebration of the Sovereign's official birthday. The setting is Horse Guards' Parade and, in rotation from year to year, the colours of one of the five Household Regiments of Foot are 'trooped' or carried. The regiments are: the Grenadier Guards, the Coldstream Guards; the Scots Guards, the Irish Guards and the Welsh Guards.

US (Golf) Open

This famous event has taken place, over various US courses, in mid-June, since 1895.

Royal Ascot Week

The racecourse was founded by Queen Anne in 1711 at Ascot in Berkshire and is subject to statutory control as part of the Crown Estates. The first race here was in August 1711 and was for Her Majesty's Plate and a hundred guineas. Until 1945, there was only the four-day Royal Meeting in June. Now there are also steeplechases and hurdles and other races bringing it up to 25 racing days a year. The Ascot Gold Cup is held on Ladies' Day, which is the Thursday of the race week and the day on which the ladies turn up in their best hats. The prestigious King George VI and Queen Elizabeth Diamond Stakes are held in July. Appropriate dress for the royal meeting is described in Chapter 11 of *History of Men's Fashion*.

Wimbledon tennis

The All England Lawn Tennis Club Championships are held six weeks before the first Monday in August, on grounds run by the All England Croquet and Lawn Tennis Club in Wimbledon, London SW19. The first championship was held in 1877 at grounds in Worple Road, Wimbledon. The last British singles winners were Fred Perry in 1936 and Virginia Wade in 1977. The biggest winner is Martina Navratilova, with nine singles' titles, who has also played more women's matches there than anyone else. It is the only Grand Slam tennis tournament played on (rye) grass. The club colours are mauve and green, adopted in 1909. The biggest men's singles' winners are William Renshaw (in Victorian times) and Pete Sampras – with seven titles each. At the first Wimbledon tournament there were 22 players and 200 spectators. The last time men wore long trousers on court was in 1939. Appropriate dress for spectators is described in Chapter 11 of *History of Men's Fashion*. As with the Chelsea Flower Show, owing to the popularity of the event, it is most advisable to book early.

Royal Academy Summer Exhibition

This exhibition of new paintings (many of which are for sale), starts at the Royal Academy in Burlington House, Piccadilly (where the Acadamy has been settled since 1868), in June and goes on until August. The contemporary paintings displayed are both from Royal Academicians (who may exhibit up to six each) and from any other artists whose works are submitted and selected for the exhibition. The Academy was founded by George III in 1764 with the dual purpose of promoting art education (through the Schools) and art exhibition. Sir Joshua Reynolds was the first President and there were thirty-four founder members (although the charter allowed for forty) to govern its affairs. The first exhibition began on 24 April 1769. There are now eighty Royal Academicians.

Royal Norfolk Show

This agricultural show takes place at the end of June.

Round Island Race

This yachting event, around the Isle of Wight, has taken place annually at the end of June, since 1931.

JULY

Henley Royal Regatta

This was started by the Henley Local Corporation in 1839 as a tourist attraction on the Thames and has been held ever since, except during the War years. Its first Royal Patron was Prince Albert, in the year of the Great Exhibition (1851). There have been four different courses. That in use today is the Straight Course, laid out in 1924 and is one mile and 550 yards long and 80 feet wide, beginning on the Berkshire side of Temple Island and finishing at Poplar point. There are two crews in each heat. The Stewards' Enclosure is open to members and their guests only and a strict dress code applies. The Mile & an Eighth Restaurant is extremely popular – so remember yet again, Book Early! The Regatta Enclosure is open to all, subject to payment and, although there is no strict dress code, many observe the spirit of the occasion. The event is normally held in late June or early July for five days, from Wednesday to Sunday. Appropriate dress for this is described in Chapter 11 of *History of Men's Fashion*.

Goodwood Festival of Speed

Also at the beginning of July is the Goodwood Festival of Speed, at Goodwood Park. The first such event took place in 1936 and it has become a regular event for historic motor cars since 1993. Also at this time, since 1886, there has been the **Eclipse Stakes** at Sandown Park, Esher, for three and four year olds.

Newmarket July Festival

This racing takes place over three days in early July.

Fowler's Match (Eton v Harrow)

This is named after a former captain of Eton College and is the last school cricket match of the season played at Lord's. The first recorded match took place in 1805 and it then became, more or less, an annual event from 1822. Other schools also play matches at Lord's but this is the most famous and most popular.

Running the Bulls in Pamplona

The spirited *encierro*, through the streets of Pamplona, takes place over eight mornings, from 8 am, during the Fiesta of San Fermin, from the second week of July. Double barriers separate participants from spectators. It seems to have started in the mid nineteenth century. If you have health and safety concerns over the dangers of cheese-rolling (or even conkers), keep well away from this as, sometimes, participants really are actually killed or injured. **Bullfighting in Spain** generally takes place between April and September and most major cities (that have not banned it), have at least one event a week; normally on a Sunday.

Royal Festival of The Horse

This takes place around 8 to 10 July at Stoneleigh Park and all the usual equestrian events take place. **The Killarney Races** have taken place around 11 to 14 July since 1947. There are National Hunt and flat races as well as other events.

The Open (Golf)

This is the British championship and it takes place, in mid-July, on one of nine famous courses, which are used in rotation: Carnoustie; Muirfield; Royal Birkdale; Royal Liverpool; Royal Lytham & St Anne's; Royal St George's; Royal

Troon; St Andrew's, and West Turnberry Resort. Once Prestwick (where the championship took place between 1860–1870); Musselburgh; Royal Cinque Ports; Prince's, and Royal Portrush were also in the rota.

BBC Proms

These concerts are held at the Royal Albert Hall between the middle of July and mid-September. The first concert of the kind to bring good music to the people was in 1895, at Queen's Hall. In 1896, Sir Henry Wood conducted the first complete season of concerts. In 1927 the BBC took over responsibility for organizing them and, as a result of the Blitzing of the Queen's Hall, the location was moved to the Royal Albert Hall in 1941.

Royal Welsh Show

This is the biggest agricultural show in Europe and takes place at Llanelwedd, Builth Wells, in mid-July.

Swan-Upping

This is the process of the taking of a census of mute swans on the river Thames in the third week of July each year. Since the twelfth century, unmarked mute swans have been the property of the Crown; although by a medieval royal charter, the Vintners' and the Dyers' Companies have also been allowed to own property in a *game* of swans. Accordingly, the swan herds of the Crown and each of these companies proceed along the river and catch the swans. The cygnets are marked (or not) according to the markings borne by their parents. The Crown's swans remain unmarked but the Vintners' swans are given two nicks in the bill (one on each side) and the Dyers' swans are given one. The birds are also checked and ringed for future reference. Once, of course, swans were eaten as part of the regal diet.

'Glorious' Goodwood

Described by King Edward VII as 'a garden party with racing tacked on', it takes place at Goodwood racecourse, over five days, at the end of July.

AUGUST

Cowes Week

This is eight days of yacht racing in the Solent, at the beginning of August, arranged by the Royal Yacht Squadron. This is a Yacht Club founded in a St James's tavern on 1 June 1815, with membership open to owners with yachts over 10 tons. The Prince Regent became a member in 1817 and, when he ascended the throne in 1820, 'Royal' was added to the name The Yacht Club. The Regatta began properly in 1826 and George IV gave a gold cup for the occasion. The name the 'Royal Yacht Squadron' dates from 1833. There are eight classes of yacht, measured according to the International Racing System: class zero comprises the biggest and class 7 comprises the smallest. Throughout the week there are cocktail parties, dinners, dances and concerts. On the final Friday there is a great display of fireworks. Important races are for the America's Cup (first raced and won by *The America* in 1851), the Admiral's Cup the Queen's Cup, the Britannia Cup and the New York Challenge Cup. The Fastnet Race is held only in odd numbered years – as it is so perilous. Appropriate dress for this is described in Chapter 11 of *History of Men's Fashion*; to which I just add that, for evening events, evening dress as indicated for particular events will conform to the descriptions of black tie and white tie in Chapter 5 of *History of Men's Fashion*.

USA PGA Championship

Normally played in mid-August, this golfing championship dates from 1916 and the prize is the Wanamaker Trophy. Two of the greatest golfing champions in this competition have been Walter Hagen in the 1920s and Jack Nicklaus between 1963 and 1980 (both with five wins). Tiger Woods has been catching up with them and, no doubt, in due course, he will get there.

Fowey Royal Regatta

Held around 14 to 20 August is the regatta of Sir Arthur Quiller-Couch's '*dearest of small cities*' , normally ending with a spectacular display of fireworks bursting over the harbour. It has been a royal event since 1907. Note that 'Fowey' rhymes with 'toy'. Yachts and dinghies come from many different places to compete in this scenic place, which is described, by the Sea Rat, in Kenneth Grahame's *The Wind in The Willows* as:

'...the little grey sea town that clings along one steep side of the harbour. There through dark doorways you look down flights of stone steps, overhung by great pink tufts of valerian and ending in a patch of sparkling blue water.'

Fowey Hall, an overblown pile on top of the hill above the town, originally built by the Hanson family and now an hotel, has been suggested as the inspiration for Toad Hall and Quiller-Couch himself is often said to have been the inspiration for the character Ratty.

Author and dramatist (creator of Peter Pan) J M Barrie wrote of Fowey 'of a moonlit night it might pass for a scene in a theatre.' If you have not been there, it certainly repays the effort. The Ship Inn is next to the church and was originally built as the town house for Philip and Alice Rashleigh, of Menabilly (which was later rented, for many years, by the writer Daphne du Maurier), and The Ship has a haunted (certainly atmospheric), room to let, which I have slept in; albeit keeping a light on!

Dartmouth Royal Regatta

This takes place around 25 to 27 August in one of the Royal Navy's most famous and scenic harbours and has been a royal event since 1856.

US Open (Tennis)

This event (dating from 1881), is one of the major tennis events and takes place between the end of August and the second week in September in New York.

Caledonian Ball

This is more fully described under the heading 'Balls' below.

SEPTEMBER

St Leger Festival

This takes place at Doncaster for nine days at the beginning of September and includes the St Leger Stakes (dating from 1776).

Goodwood Revival Meeting

This takes place around 16 to 18 September and there are motoring events involving cars built between 1948 and 1966.

Opening Night of the Metropolitan Opera

Towards the end of September is the opening night of the Metropolitan Opera at the Lincoln Center in New York.

OCTOBER

Prix de l'Arc de Triomphe

This is an 'all ages' flat race over a one and a half mile course; which has been held, since 1920, in early October, at Longchamp, in tribute to the French soldiers who died in the First World War.

Champions' Day, Newmarket

This comprises six Group flat races in mid-October.

NOVEMBER

Brazilian Formula One Grand Prix

This takes place in early November at the Interlagos Autodromo in São Paulo, in its current form since 1990; although the original track dates back to 1940.

RAC London to Brighton Veteran Car Run

This is a delightful annual event for which cars come from all over the world to participate. Annually (except for War years), since 1927 qualifying cars have set off from Hyde Park Corner at sunrise, on the first Sunday in November, and run down to Marine Parade in Brighton. The first actual run took place on 14th November 1896 and was called *The Emancipation Run*, to celebrate the enactment of *The Locomotives On The Highway Act*, which raised the speed limit from 4 mph to 14 mph. The need for a man to walk with a red flag in front of a motor vehicle had already been abolished but, before the 1896 run, a red flag was ceremonially burned.

Qualifying vehicles now must have been built before 31 December 1904.

The Open, Cheltenham

This event, comprising jump races, takes place over three days in mid-November.

The Lord Mayor's Show

The Lord Mayor of the City of London is an ancient office which currently dates from a royal charter from King John in 1215 (the same year as Magna Carta); although the first recorded office holder is actually Henry Fitz-Ailwyn in 1189. Altogether seven hundred men and one woman have held the office (which is an annual office by election of 'Common Hall': comprising all liverymen of one year's standing or more, and certain City office-holders; all aldermen who have served as Sheriff are eligible to stand). In November, the Lord Mayor progresses in a parade in which his coach is the principal vehicle, from his official residence in the Mansion House in the City of London, to the Royal Courts of Justice in Strand, via a service of blessing in St Paul's Cathedral. In the Courts, he swears allegiance to the Sovereign and then progresses back. The most famous Lord Mayor is probably Sir Richard (Dick) Whittington who was in fact a mercer (cloth merchant); apparently, he did not (according to an urban legend, with a black cat) find his fortune by ridding the King of the Barbary Coast of a plague of rats! There is, though, an ancient stone monument to him (called *The Whittington Stone*) at the foot of Highgate Hill (including a stone cat), marking the spot where he is supposed to have turned back again to the City.

DECEMBER

Opening Night of La Scala, Milan

This opening night of one of the world's great opera houses has taken place on the Feast of St Ambrose, since 1778.

Varsity Rugby Match

This has taken place, since 1872, between the rugby teams of Oxford and Cambridge Universities. Since 1921 it has been at Twickenham Stadium (also known as 'Twickers'), the home of rugby football in Middlesex. The Stadium was built on ground formerly used as a cabbage patch and so, sometimes, it is also called 'Cabbage Patch'. Nowadays, cauliflower-ears are the only vegetables produced there.

The first game there was played on 2 October 1909 between Harlequins and Richmond. The first international was on 15 January 1910 between England and Wales.

Rugby football is supposed to have been invented by a bored schoolboy at Rugby School. A plaque in the school reads:

> This stone commemorates the exploit of
> William Webb Ellis
> Who with a fine disregard for the rules of football
> As played in his time
> First took the ball in his arms and ran with it
> thus originating the distinctive feature of
> the rugby game.
>
> AD 1823.

Rugby School is in Warwickshire and was founded in 1567 by the will of Lawrence Sheriff, originally to educate the poor of the area. It is now one of England's major public schools. Its most famous headmaster was Dr Thomas Arnold (1795–1842) who introduced enlightened reforms in education; emphasizing sport, self-control, reliability, steadfastness and taught the assumption of responsibility which, altogether, proved a combination that has since been adopted in education systems throughout the world. Suggestions for dress to spectate are set out in Chapter 11 of *History of Men's Fashion*.

Hogmanay

This also is principally a Scottish festivity on New Year's Eve, with much singing and dancing and more Scotch whisky; a repeat of *Auld Lang Syne* and then it's back on with those snow shoes.

Activities and events without particular seasons

Balls

George Bernard Shaw once observed that *'dancing is the perpendicular expression of a horizontal desire.'* Plainly, GBS had not been reading Sir Richard Burton's versions of Cheikh Nefzaoui's *The Perfumed Garden* or the *Kama Sutra* of Vatsyayana, in which there is plenty of description of variously angled expressions of this desire.

Some balls are arranged privately (most notably the University Balls) but Queen Charlotte's Ball and such like are no longer held and there is no official control of what events are, or are not, a part of the Season (to the extent that it survives at all, following HM The Queen's abolition of the presentation of Debutantes in 1958). There is a group called The London Season, which holds itself out as representing 'Society' and arranges functions for wannabees. The champagne house of Veuve Cliquot publishes annual cards on which *its* idea of the London Season is promulgated (as well as an advertisement for its wares).

There is still, notably, the Caledonian Ball, which has taken place (except during years such as wartime), at the end of April each year since 1840, originally under the patronage of the Duke and Duchess of Atholl, who started the ball. Since 1849, it has been a subscription ball with the proceeds going to charity. Now it is held at Grosvenor House and there is a dinner followed by much Highland dancing and high revelry; including set reels, and a strict dress code prevails, comprising full Highland Dress, mess dress or dress coats and white tie; dinner jackets are *not* permitted. The ladies wear ball gowns. Decorations and tiaras (for those entitled to them) are encouraged!

The Oban Ball is another old event that takes place at the end of August in the Oban Gathering Hall, for those prepared to make the long trip down there. Again, the same strict dress code applies.

The Inns of Court (chiefly famous for the Gray's Inn Ball and The Middle Temple Revels, which are summer events), seem to have been keeping a low public profile since news reports, on June 23 2000, in *The Independent* newspaper, of routine drunkenness and hooliganism amongst barristers at these events.

Scotch reels, cotillions (an early French import), together with English and Scotch country dances, were the main dances at British balls until the French quadrille was introduced in around 1813. Amongst others, there also came: the Viennese Waltz (originally dating from the second half of the eighteenth century); danced in a fast time and with each pair in more open holds than now and probably brought to England around the same time as the French quadrille; becoming in England, gradually modified into the wholly closed, sweeping, slow

Waltz, in which each pair is independent of all the other dancers and, for this anti-social aspect, execrated by some, including Lord Byron, in his poem *The Waltz*, ending :

> Voluptuous Waltz! And dare I thus blaspheme?
> Thy bard forgot thy praises were his theme.

Then there is the polka (devised by a bored peasant girl in Bohemia one Sunday afternoon in 1834; introduced to Prague ballrooms in 1835 and brought to England in the mid-nineteenth century).

Then, of course, there came all the subsequent dances, from the military two step (an English dance from 1900); the foxtrot (dating from 1914, originally called the 'bunny-hug'); the charleston (named for Charleston in South Carolina and dating from 1923) and then all the Latin American dances: such as the tango, evolving between 1850 and 1880 in Uruguay and Argentina, originally as a slum dance but also becoming a dance of the social élite from 1910 and famously popularized in the USA and Europe by Rudolph Valentino, who danced a slow tango magnificently in the 1921 film *The Four Horsemen of the Apocalypse*. What makes the scene specially remarkable now is that his dancing partner, Beatrice Dominguez (1896–1921) died of peritonitus (as would Valentino in 1926), before the film was even released.

Rudolph Valentino (born Rodolfo Alphonso Raffaello Piero Filiberto Guglielmi 1895–1926) was one of the first great stars of the (silent) screen; starring in films such as *The Four Horsemen of The Apocalyse*; *The Sheikh* and *Son of the Sheikh*. Although they are over-acted in a wide-eyed, over-demonstrative way and even though the footage is black and white and old and crackling, it is still possible to see the star that briefly shone. Rather like Cary Grant, even now, most people have heard of Rudolph Valentino and even recognize him. The suggestion that his voice was unlikely to have carried him into the age of the talkies is wholly unsupported by the recordings that exist of it, including him singing *A Kashmiri Love Song* in a pleasing baritone. The feverish, on-screen adulation which he inspired was not reflected in his personal life. Twice married and twice divorced, he did not seem to find and keep any woman; indeed, he said: 'Women are not in love with me; I am just the canvass upon which they paint their dreams.' When he died, at 31, of peritonitis, following an operation for a gastric ulcer, the public mourning was great and the streets of New York were lined with hundreds of thousands of weeping mourners; albeit that this outpouring was encouraged by the studio, which had yet to release his last film. The anniversary of his death is still marked at the mausoleum where he was entombed in a vault originally reserved for the husband of his friend June

Mathis. The vault was, at first, 'borrowed' and later quietly bought by his estate. Legend has it that he was buried still wearing the platinum slave bracelet and watch given to him by his second wife, set designer Natacha Rambova (actually born 'Winifred Shaughnessy'). For many years, following his death, a mysterious 'lady in black' used to appear at this annual ceremony.

He was not, in fact, originally, the poor Italian boy of popular fancy but the son of a veterinary surgeon. Owing to his French mother, he spoke French as well as Italian and also learned English and Spanish and had some knowledge of German. The catalogue of the sale of his effects, following his death, shows that he had an extensive library and many valuable, even museum quality, antiques – especially furniture, doors, paintings, arms and armour (which he brought from his European tours), as well as the latest motor cars and four Arabian horses. Everything was sold off for a song to pay debts, following his death. His life was a far cry from following the cult of ignorance which governs the tastes and values of most modern celebrities. His former house (in a Spanish style) *Falcon Lair*, above Beverly Hills, has, fairly recently, been stripped of most of the cladding materials and the site will probably become a 'condo' – in the best modern taste.

Another dance is the paso doble (Spanish for 'two step' and modelled somewhat on the bullfight's ritualized dance of death; this dance dates from 1920); the rumba (originally from Cuba and brought to Europe and the USA in the 1930s); the cha-cha-cha (from Cuba and popularized from 1952); the bossa nova (dating from its origination in 1958 in Rio de Janeiro) and the jive, reaching its zenith in the 1950s and 1960s;

Besides all these, there is the famous Brazilian samba, of African origin, which is at the core of the Rio de Janeiro Carnaval, and has been for around a hundred years; the forms vary, including Baion and Marcha. There is the ballroom or Carioca samba, deriving from the rocking samba. Before 1914, the samba was generally called the Maxixe (indeed, there are references to this word well after 1914). The dance was introduced to world audiences in 1933, by Fred Astaire and Dolores Del Rio (one of the nearly forgotten great Hollywood beauties), in the film *Flying Down to Rio* and, in 1941, Carmen Miranda performed it in *That Night in Rio*; the modern classic tune is Ary Barroso's *Brasil*. The ballroom samba, combining rapid steps on the quarter beat, with the samba tic (pelvic movement), together with a swaying motion, is more difficult to perform well than most other ballroom dances.

After these, there came the twist and various disco-dances, in which there is not even contact between partners, let alone any wider social participation: it's all just head-banging and shakin' it to beep, beep, bop and za, boom, boom, boom.

Unless otherwise stated on the invitation, correct dress for formal balls is full evening dress, as described in Chapter 5 of *History of Men's Fashion*. However, for some events, such as the Middle Temple 'Revels', which had already declined to black tie and dinner jacket, you now just need to wear a lounge suit. If you attend a ball which is preceded by a dinner, be sure that you ask your immediate female dinner neighbours for the pleasure of a dance and, if you have a hostess, be sure to ask her and her daughters too.

Billiards

> To play billiards well is a sign of a misspent youth.
>
> Charles Roupell

The games in the Billiard family of games have been played in some form since time immemorial and do, probably, derive from the earliest forms of Croquet and the name 'Billiards' itself might well derive from either the old French *billart* (for 'mace') or *bille* (for 'ball'). Other very old games, which are probably unrelated to Billiards are Skittles (ten pin bowling); Quoits and Tennis.. Ground Billiards was the main game between the 1340s and the 1600s. Port and King Billiards were played on a table and green baize came to be the cloth on the table to remind of the grass from which the game came. An inventory tells us that King Louis XI had a billiard table (long before Louis XIV was supposed to have invented the game (see page 70). In sixteenth century Britain the Duke of Norfolk and the Earl of Leicester had billiard tables and there was a billiard table close by as Mary Queen of Scots awaited her execution. Table billiards was very popular in France and Britain by the seventeenth century. The first rules for the game were settled by Charles Cotton in his *The Compleat Gamester* of 1674, when the pockets were actually hazards and not goals. The balls were hit with a mace but, gradually, the narrower tail of the mace was used to strike the balls. 'Tail' in French is *queue* hence eventually 'cue'. In 1807 a French political prisoner, called François Mingaud, whiling away his time in jug with billiards, became frustrated at the way that his cue kept slipping off the ball and came up with the leather cue tip. Snooker was a game that was developed in India under the British Raj. French Carambole came into existence in the eighteenth century (Carambola in Spain and Portugal), and American Pool was developed following independence (that is pocket billiards; whereas Carom Billiards is played with no pockets); Pin Billiards became an Italian and South American variation.

Boxing

Float like a butterfly; sting like a bee!

Muhammad Ali

High Cecil Lowther, 5th Earl of Lonsdale (1857–1944) was a great sportsman and extravagant eccentric who had run away as youngster, joined a circus as an acrobat in Switzerland and then travelled to the USA to be a cowboy; even holding up the Denver stage coach, as a prank. He was known as the 'Yellow Earl' because, according to *Time* magazine for 18 June 1934, 'Yellow are the racing colours, the motor cars and the silk hats of footmen in the service of the Yellow Earl, Britain's beloved sporting peer the Earl of Lonsdale.' Apart from racing and hunting, the Yellow Earl was keen on boxing and the National Sporting Club, of which he was patron, introduced the Lonsdale belts in his honour. These are the oldest championship belts in boxing and date from 1909. Originally a belt was awarded to each champion of each weight division. A winner could keep it if he won it and defended it twice. Sir Henry Cooper (born 1935) was the first to win three outright. Muhammad Ali (then called Cassius Clay) said on television of Cooper's knockdown of him at their non-title fight in 1963 that Cooper had hit him so hard that his 'ancestors in Africa felt it!' Now you have to win and defend three times. The first heavyweight belt was won by Bombadier Billy Wells in 1911. He defended it thirteen times. That belt is made of 22ct gold and enamel and is now kept in the Royal Artillery Barracks at Woolwich in South London. Later Billy Wells was one of the men to strike the gong at the beginning of J Arthur Rank films.

Cards

I am very sorry that I have not learned to play at cards. It is very useful in life: it generates kindness and consolidates society.

Dr Samuel Johnson

Always remember the legal defamation case of **Gordon-Cumming -v- Wilson & Others**, which resulted, in June 1891, from 'The Royal Baccarat Scandal' (otherwise known as the *Tranby Croft Affair*, after the place where it occurred). The then Prince of Wales (later Edward VII), had been present at a house party in the house of shipping magnate Sir Arthur Wilson in September

129

1890. To please him, the host arranged for everyone to play the Prince of Wales's favourite card game – what was then the illegal card game of Baccarat. Another guest, Sir William Gordon-Cumming, was accused of cheating by several guests. They said that he had surreptitiously adjusted his bets after the cards had been dealt from the shoe (card box). Gordon-Cumming signed a virtual confession in return for silence and he promised not to play cards again. He then brought an action for defamation, as a result of the circulation of rumours (probably begun by a Royal favourite and notorious gossip, Lady Daisy – 'Babbling' – Brooke), that he was a card cheat. He forced the Prince of Wales (who was not a Defendant to the case) to testify. The Prince of Wales gave evidence that he had played the (illegal) game and that he had not reported Gordon-Cumming to his regiment for cheating. However, the overall evidence (including the confession), against the Plaintiff was too much and he lost his case and became a recluse in Scotland with his new wife. The Prince moved on from Baccarat to the games of Bridge and Whist.

Just as they say that there is no sound quite so satisfying as the sound of crashing glass, one of the greatest of social sins is cheating at cards and many regard it as much worse than adultery.

Playing cards seem to have been developed in China before the beginning of the thirteenth century and other playing cards were known in Europe during the fourteenth century. How European cards developed is subject to several theories but it seems most likely that the Mameluke Empire of Egypt introduced their decks of cards comprising four suits of thirteen cards (with ten numbered cards and three court cards in each suit). Such cards were known in Europe in 1371 and specifically in France by 1392 as Charles VI bought some in that year. In fact those decks had fourteen cards in each of four suits. The suits of spades, clubs, diamonds, and hearts seem to have been devised in the fifteenth century in France for piquet. By this time, playing card games had become established in England and there was even legislation there in 1462 to ban cards and the prohibition continued on into the nineteenth century. Colonial expansion popularized the French and English card formats across the world.

This is no book in which to describe the complex rules of any of the thousands of known card games but it is worth mentioning the names of some of them to stir up interest: contract bridge; whist; baccarat and chemin de fer; blackjack; euchre; faro; piquet; pinocle; cribbage; gin rummy; bezique; poker; canasta; black Maria, and patience. For more on the history of this subject, a good starting point is the book by David Parlett, listed in the Bibliography.

The Village Fête

There can be nothing more redolent of the English summer than the Village Fête. Charity stalls with tombolas and bric-a- brac, cakes, cakes and more cakes, entertainers for children, morris dancers, and the inevitable tea tent, well pegged against the possibility of a rainy Saturday.

On a grander scale, the Agricultural Show is to be found in towns and villages where farming is not simply an entertainment or has been taken over by agri-businesses. The longest and most elegant carrots having been measured; prizes awarded for the best parsnip wine and maderia cake, and the welly-throwing conclusively won for the third year in a row, the beer tent is now bulging.

Ice Skating

> In skating over thin ice, our safety is in our speed.
>
> Ralph Waldo Emerson

Ice skating is to be had in several places throughout the winter months. Amongst the splendid venues are: outside L'Hotel de Ville in Paris; at the Natural History Museum in South Kensington; on a rink at Somerset House in the Strand; a rink near Winchester Cathedral; one at Hampton Court Palace; another at the Tower of London; one at the Royal Pavilion, Brighton as well as rinks at York, Cardiff, Glasgow and Edinburgh.

The Turf and Seasons for Flats and Steeple Chases

> O, for a horse with wings!
>
> William Shakespeare

Racing: The world's thoroughbred race horses derive from the breeding from three Foundation Sires: the Godolphin Arabian (owner Francis, Lord Godolphin); the Darley Arabian (owner Thomas Darley), and the Byerley Turk (owner Captain Robert Byerley). These horses (briefly described below) were crossed with English mares, for the purpose of combining the qualities of form, endurance, intelligence and heart and lung capacity of the Arabians with the larger size of the English stock. The modern thoroughbred is the result.

Their lines, down to the present day, are recorded in the General Stud Book, begun by James Weatherby in 1791, when he recorded over three hundred and fifty mares that were descended from Matchem (in the Godolphin line); Eclipse (in the Darley line), and Herod (in the Bryerley line). Weatherby's still maintains the Stud Book.

Arabian Horses

The Arabian horse (*Equus agilis*) originating in the Middle East, is probably the earliest type of horse used by man, for anything apart from food. Arabian legend holds that they are sprung from the great-great grandson of Noah; and they have always been prized by the Bedouin, for their beauty, intelligence and endurance, over distance and in harsh conditions. Their typical characteristics include a short back (with twenty-three vertebrae instead of twenty-four), small heads (with a broad prominent forehead, 'Jibbah', holding the blessings of Allah), and dished faces, big eyes, wide jowls, delicate muzzles and smallish, well-shaped ears, as well as a long, arched neck and high crest ('Mitbah'), denoting much courage; they have large, flared, efficient nostrils and great lung capacity. The carriage of their tails shows pride and they are especially noted for their floating, phantom-like movement. Probably a little smaller in ancient history, pure-bred Arabians now make around fifteen hands in height.

There are cave paintings in France that have been dated to 17,000 years ago showing that, even then, horses were known to man but as quarry. The nomadic Bedouin had mastered Arabian horses by around 1500 BC; preferring mares for riding in their raids ('ghazus'), since, as a singular exception in their line of descent from Noah, the females are quieter than the males. They are well represented in the literature and art of ancient civilizations and military commanders, from Alexander the Great to Napoleon, rode Arabian horses.

The Duke of Wellington's horse, Copenhagen though was a thoroughbred, whose dam had been Lady Catherine (a Stud Book half-bred thoroughbred/Arabian), and he was by Meteor, son of the famous Eclipse. He was born after the Battle of Copenhagen in 1807, at which he had been *in utero*. The saddle that carried Wellington into the Battle of Waterloo was a Gidden's saddle, from the saddler which was founded in 1806 and, now owned by Schneider's Boots, also deals in riding and hunting equipment and clothes and fine leather goods. Copenhagen died in 1836 and was buried under a Turkey oak on the Duke's estate. The Duke was later asked by the War Museum to allow Copenhagen's skeleton to stand next to that of Napoleon's equally brave (and often wounded) Arabian mount, Morengo, (which had died in 1837) but the Duke (no doubt remembering that he had once said of Copenhagen: "There may have been faster horses, no doubt many handsomer, but for bottom and endurance, I never saw his fellow", and that he had carried Wellington to Downing Street when he had become Prime Minister in 1828), allowed his old friend to rest on. The second Duke erected a commemorative stone to him and a hoof that had been stolen by a servant before the burial was eventually returned and made into an inkstand. One of Morengo's hoofs was made into a snuff box in the Brigade of Guards.

Pure Arabian horses *Al Khamsa* comprises five principal families: *Kehilan, Seglawi, Abeyan, Hamdani* and *Habdan*. The Bedouin jealously guarded the purity of the strain and, to prevent too much inbreeding, brought in new (but still pure) blood from horses captured in battle and in their raids. These horses, especially the mares, very seldom otherwise changed hands, except as honourable gifts.

Besides these strict bloodlines, there are now Arabian horses that may be further described, depending on the name of the country or breeder of their later breeding, such as: Crabbett; Davenport; Egyptian; Straight Egyptian; English; Kellogg; as well as hybrids between them in various degrees.

Wilfred and Lady Anne Blunt visited Arabia in 1881 and took 29 mares and stallions back to their estate in Britain where they formed the Crabbett Stud and, from this, offspring were generated that have gone the world around.

After earlier attempts at breeding Arabian horses in the USA, adversely affected by the American Civil War, Ulysses S Grant took gifts of horses back from Arabia to the USA. After the Chicago World Fair, in 1893, there was purchase of Turkish stock and in 1906 America began its own Registration of Arabian blood horses, following Homer Davenport's importation of desert-bred stock and 1908 saw the establishment of a Stud Book. From all of this has developed the largest number of Arabian horses in any country.

The Foundation Sires

The brief history of the Godolphin Arabian (sometimes called the 'Barb'), is as follows. An Arabian horse, standing at 15 hands, foaled around 1724, was the gift of the Bey of Tunis to the King of France. After he had changed hands several times, eventually, he was brought to England by Edward Coke in 1729. There is no evidence to support the romance that he was redeemed from pulling a cart. Coke died in 1733 and left a colt by the Arabian, named Lath, and Lath's dam Roxana to Francis, 2nd Earl of Godolphin (1678–1766) who was a founder of the Foundling Hospital (orphanage) in London and Lord Privy Seal (Keeper of the Sovereign's personal seal). Coke's stallions, including the Arabian, Hobgoblin and Whitefoot, he left to another friend, Roger Williams. That same year Godolphin bought the Arabian, soon to be known as the Godolphin Arabian, and moved him to his stables inside Wandlebury Ring, an Iron Age fort near Newmarket, which is a market town in Suffolk, where there has been racing since 1174. The first cup race was in 1634, for a cup donated by King Charles I. It is, besides the site of a racecourse, the home to the Jockey Club clubhouse and Tattersalls' – auctioneers of bloodstock.

At Newmarket, the Godolphin Arabian sired a large and notable progeny; the most influential possibly being Cade in 1734, from the descendants of which came, for example, the famous Gimcrack (painted by George Stubbs (1724–1806)). The descendants from this line have had a large impact on thoroughbred horse breeding throughout the world. The Godolphin Arabian died in 1753; being buried with a commemorative stone under the archway of the stable block, which can still be seen.

However, the Godolphin Arabian's line has been less influential than the Darley Arabian's (the last horse in the Godolphin line to win the Epsom Derby was Santa Claus in 1964).

The Darley Arabian was foaled around 1700 and from Eclipse in his line are descended about eighty per cent of the world's thoroughbreds. Eclipse was foaled in 1764 and named after a great eclipse of the sun that happened in that year. He won eighteen races, many of them a walk-over and he was retired to stud in 1771. His skeleton is on display in the Horseracing Museum at Newmarket.

The Bryerley Turk was foaled in about 1680 and also has less influence on modern stock than the Darley Arabian.

Another famous horse grave is of course that of Red Rum (1965–1995) record thrice winner of the Grand National (1973, 1974 and 1977). He is buried by the winning post at Aintree. The grave of the Aga Khan's Shergar (1978– kidnapped in Ireland in 1983), which (having slowed to an exercise canter towards the end), won the 1981 Epsom Derby by a record ten lengths, is not known. The jockey on the runner-up in that race thought that he had satisfied his life's ambition by winning the Derby until: 'I saw another horse on the horizon'. The footage of this race is spectacular and ten lengths is a record of margin that still stands for the Epsom Derby. In 1981 Shergar also won the Irish Derby Stakes and the King George VI and Queen Elizabeth Stakes. In fact, the previous record for the *fastest* Epsom Derby win was broken in 2010 by Workforce.

Types of Races and Famous Racing Events

Types of Races

There are many types of races but, broadly, half are Handicap races and half are Stakes races. Further specification is as follows:

Type of race Description

Group – 1,2,3; the highest types.

Listed – the next highest types.

Rated Stakes – valuable handicaps with 10–14 pound weight range.

Conditions Stakes – races for horses below class A.

Classified Stakes – races with the maximum rating for horses that have raced more than three times or twice and won at least once.

Handicap – races where the weight to be carried is determined by the official handicapper.

Nursery – Handicap race for two year olds.

Maiden Handicap – races for three year old maidens with a maximum rating of 70 that have run at least four times.

Maiden – races for horses that have never won a race.

Rated Maiden – Maiden races with a maximum rating for horses that have run at least three times.

Novice – races for two year olds that have won no more than twice.

Auction Maiden – races for two year olds originally sold in specified auctions.

Median Auction Maiden – races for two year olds by stallions which have established a median price for yearlings at specified sales.

Selling – races for low class horses where the horses (especially the winners) are auctioned.

Claiming – races with an allocation of weight according to the Claiming Price; the lower the weight the lower the Claiming Price.

Apprentice – races for apprentice jockeys only.

Amateur – races for Amateurs only.

Lady – races for female apprentice jockeys and amateurs.

Gentlemen – races for male amateurs only.

Note: '*Claiming Price*' means the price for horses that are offered for sale before the start of the race; and '*Maximum Rating*' means a horse's rating, according to previous race performance and this applies in the UK and Ireland to horses previously raced in the UK and Ireland so horses that have been raced only in other countries (however successfully) will be rated first out in the UK and Ireland at zero.

Flat racing

Classics

There are five classic races, for three year olds: in the first week in May there is the Newmarket 2000 Guinea Stakes and, on the first weekend, there is the

Newmarket 1000 Guineas. The Epsom Oaks takes place at Epsom in the first week in June and the Derby takes place on the Saturday. The fifth classic flat race is the St Leger at Doncaster in the second weekend in September.

Only two horses have ever won the 'Triple Crown' which is the 2000 Guineas, the Derby and the St Leger: Bahram (owned by the Aga Khan) did it in 1935 and Nijinsky in 1970 (owned by Charles W Engelhard Jr, said by *The Times* to be the metals' tycoon on whom Ian Fleming based Auric Goldfinger; although the name derives from the 'brutalist' architect and uglifier Ernö Goldfinger; whereas Goldfinger strongly objected to the use of his name, Engelhard was actually delighted with the characterization).

Other important flat races and events
These include the Lincoln Handicap, at Doncaster, at the end of March and then the St James Guinness Festival at Newmarket in early May; Royal Ascot in mid-June; the Sandown Coral Eclipse Stakes in early July; King George Day at Ascot towards the end of July; 'Glorious' Goodwood at the end of July and beginning of August; the Racing Post Trophy Meeting at Doncaster ends the season in mid-October.

Jump racing

These are split between hurdles and steeple-chases and, mixed in too are flat bumper races organized at National Hunt level. These all take place from Autumn through to the Spring. For the hurdles, there are juvenile, novice and open races and steeple-chases comprise novice and open races. Each category has a championship race at the Cheltenham Festival and John Smith's Aintree Grand National Meeting. Cheltenham takes place in early March and culminates in the famous Cheltenham Gold Cup. The Aintree Grand National (surely the world's most famous horse race), takes place in early April.

Correct dress for the various racing events (including the Derby) is described in Chapter 11 of *History of Men's Fashion*.

Basics on horse betting

An 'odds against' bet is a bet that an event such as a particular horse winning a particular race is expressed as figures such as 2:1 against, which means that if you bet £1 and the horse wins, you win £2 plus the return of your stake.

An 'odds-on' bet means that the bookies reckon that it is more likely than not that an event will happen so if the odds are 1:2-on, it means that for every two pounds that you stake, you will receive one pound plus the return of the original stake. The fact that the bookies place these odds this way does not mean that, objectively, it is more likely than not that the event will happen as they forecast.

An 'each way' bet is in fact two bets of equal size. The first is a bet to win at the odds offered (as above) and the second is a place bet that the horse will come in (say) the first three. The place bet pays at a fraction of the overall odds 'a place'. But this does mean that if the horse wins, you have two winning bets: the 'to win' bet and the first place 'place' bet.

Multiple bets come as doubles or triples or accumulators. A double or a triple means that you bet on two or three events and both need to win to pay out. An accumulator is a succession of 'to win' bets where all the winnings from the previous event are staked on the next until the final event is won or the stake is lost.

There are many other types of bets too but these are beyond the scope of this book.

Finally, a new type of betting system has been introduced called 'bet 365', which means that, if the odds are 3:1 when you place your bet but they later move to 2:1, your bet is preserved at 3:1 but if the odds lengthen to say 6:1, you get the benefit of that, so if the horse wins, you are paid out at six times your stake and not just three times. For anyone who wants to know more about this or indeed betting and gambling generally, try John Scarne's book, mentioned in the Bibliography.

For those who want news and events in the racing world there is *The Racing Post*.

London Opera and Ballet

Opera is when a guy gets stabbed in the back and, instead of bleeding, he sings.

Ed Gardner

The Royal Opera House, Covent Garden: is now home to the Royal Opera and the Royal Ballet as well as the Orchestra of the Royal Opera House. The façade and the auditorium date from the 1858 construction. The rest dates from a reconstruction in the 1990s. It began as the Theatre Royal Covent Garden by Letters Patent granted on his restoration by Charles II to Sir William Davenant. A new building went up on the site of a former *convent garden* in 1728 for John Rich. The building was used for drama for a long time. The clown Joseph Grimaldi (1778–1837) introduced the modern clown and the pantomime dame there in sing-alongs with the audience. In 1846 the opera and ballet companies moved from Her Majesty's Theatre, Haymarket, which had previously been the main home of opera and ballet in London. The Covent Garden building was remodelled in 1847. Following a fire, it was rebuilt again in 1858 and became known as the Royal Opera House in 1892. A long overdue internal reconstruction was completed in the 1990s. All the modern greats of Opera and Ballet have appeared here. What is now called Her Majesty's Theatre has been on or near its present site since 1705; previously known as the Haymarket Opera House and the Italian Opera House. The old theatre was destroyed by fire in 1867. The only part of the original Nash and Repton development to survive is the atmospheric Royal Opera Arcade (formerly Market Lane), which links Pall Mall and Charles II Street. There are summer and winter seasons for opera and ballet. Suggested dress for the opera and ballet is given in Chapter 11 of *History of Men's Fashion*.

The Sadler's Wells' Theatre also has a long and interesting history. Around 1683 a well was found in the garden of Richard Sadler's property, *The Musick House*. A canny entrepreneur, he marketed the water as possessing medicinal properties and was backed by a Fellow of the College of Physicians. It quickly became fashionable as a venue and Sadler introduced musical entertainment for his patrons. Between 1699 and 1790, as a result of the brewing of beer from the water, it attracted the description: 'the nursery of debauchery'. Despite the fact that the Theatres Royal enjoyed a monopoly over theatrical productions at this time, their productions were limited to the autumn and winter and so (a blind eye turned to it), Sadler's Wells, gave performances outside these seasons with summer opera productions. Between 1801 and 1825, Edmund Kean started here as a boy actor and Joseph Grimaldi began here as a dancer. Indeed, Grimaldi's last stage performance was at Sadler's Wells in 1828. The arrival of Samuel Phelps and the passing of the Theatres Act 1843 gave rise to the opportunity to mount stage productions of Shakespeare's plays. However, following this period of prosperity, there was a low point for seventy years after 1862 and the theatre was used for roller skating, science festivals, music hall and even early silent films. In 1925, Lilian Bayliss of the Old Vic formed a committee of The Great and The Good to raise funds to buy the theatre for the nation. This was achieved and a new theatre opened in January 1931. This was twinned in productions with the Old Vic and even the stages were the same size to allow the removal of scenery from one to the other. Ninette de Valois's influence (which also extended to the founding of the Royal Ballet and the Royal Ballet School), gave rise to the worldwide fame for dance and the theatre became principally concerned with opera and ballet. The opera company moved to the English National Opera at the Coliseum in 1968 and the 1970s saw a diversity of performance. The old theatre closed in June 1996 and a new theatre opened on the site in 1998, and goes from strength to strength.

Concerts

There are many great concert halls in London: the Southbank Centre has The Royal Festival Hall, the Purcell Room and the Queen Elizabeth Hall; there is the Barbican Centre; the Wigmore Hall; the Royal Albert Hall and the new Cadogan Hall, as well as St John's Smith Square and King's Place. The newspapers and of course the internet have listings for what's on.

CHAPTER 9

Road, Rail and Sea Travel and Living Abroad

To travel hopefully is better than to arrive, and the true success is to labour.

Robert Louis Stevenson

Introduction

This is not a coffee-table book about cars, trains or ships and so what follow are strictly personal views, intended to stir up enthusiasm for travel, rather than any kind of guide to vehicles and vessels.

Road

My favourite motor car in the spirit of the Gran Turismo motor cars is the 1931 8 litre Bentley (coachwork by HJ Mulliner): the last great creation of Bentley under Walter Owen Bentley ('WO'). It was manufactured and marketed to be the biggest British road motor car to date and presented serious rivalry for Rolls Royce. Only one hundred were built. As a result of the depression, the company fell into financial difficulties but, because of its cars' five *Le Mans* wins and, maybe because of the *Blue Train Bentley*, it was rescued by Rolls Royce. Star of stage and screen Jack Buchanan had a 1931 eight litre Bentley, which was the first road model produced, and it is illustrated in Plate 27. Buchanan used to mount *Bonzo* mascots on his cars' radiators, such as that illustrated in Plate 28 and they are still made by Louis Lejeune Ltd. *Bonzo* was a popular cartoon dog creation of George E Studdy and first appeared in *The Sketch* magazine in 1922.

The Blue Train Bentley

'Bentley Boy' Woolf Barnato was the man who bet over dinner in the Carlton Hotel in Cannes, one evening in 1930, that he could drive his ordinary Speed Six Bentley saloon (with coachwork by HJ Mulliner) and race against the Blue Train (Le Calais-Mediterranée Express), from Cannes, and that he could be in his London club before the Blue Train reached Calais. Racing all night, he reached his club, in St James's Street, four minutes before the Blue Train did reach Calais; for which he was then fined for speeding by the French authorities! But it is a race that will live on in motoring history.

The Silent Sportscar and a Fabulous Modern Machine

Another wonderful car is the 1939 Mark V 4.75 litre Bentley Sports Saloon (coachwork by Park Ward), the 'Derby Bentleys' were the first Rolls Royce-made Bentley motor cars. The Derby was also known as 'The Silent Sports' Car'; presumably, from the fact that it lacked the engine noise of the earlier Bentleys.

Of course, few people would actually want to travel long distances in an old car; lacking 'sat-nav'; air conditioning and all the rest of it and, if you want to travel in a hurry, the modern Bristol Fighter T, shown in Plate 29 might take some beating.

Bristol cars had begun production after the Second World War, as a result of a down-turn in the need for airplanes which the Bristol Aeroplane Company had produced to that point; including the Brisfit, the Blenheim and the Beaufighter. Their Olympus engine, originally designed for the Vulcan bomber, was later famously modified for Concorde. The first Bristol motor car was the Type 400. However, the car division became a wholly owned subsidiary of the main company in 1956. It was taken into private hands in 1961 by Sir George White and Mr TAD Crook – and this, British motor car company continues to this day producing a small number of handmade, elegantly under-stated, performance touring cars; the latest of which are the Blenheim 3, 3S and SG but there is also the sports Bristol Fighter, which began production in 2004 and reaches approximately 210 mph with a V10 7,996 cc engine and has an acceleration from 0–60 in 4 seconds. There is also the more powerful Fighter T. There must be worse ways in which to spend around a quarter of a million pounds. It has a claimed top speed of 270 mph.

There was an earlier Zagato-bodied Bristol motor car: the Bristol 406 (with coachwork by the Italian coach-maker Zagato); this was the last Bristol motor car to carry the 2 litre Filton-built engine (stretched to 2.216 litres). There were six special-bodied saloons and one coupé on which Zagato made the coachwork.

The Bristol Blenheim Speedster is a modern interpretation of a 1950s prototype sports car, known as the Bullet. The original was never put into production. However, the car was used for tests until the 1970s, when it was laid up and forgotten. Re-discovered in the 1990s, it was restored. Bristol Cars will make a small number of up-dated reproductions to special order. The price is not advertised. Like so many great things, if one needs to ask the price, one probably cannot afford it. The new car is called the Speedster and is based on the Bristol Blenheim chassis and drive train. The car carries a 5,900 cc V8 engine, accelerates from 0–60 in an impressive 5 seconds and has a top speed of 160 mph.

Rail

I like railways and travel by train because it retains an element of romance for me that is lacking in road transport. I especially like solitary train journeys; time to think, to savour the expectation of arriving. Yes, Stevenson was certainly right.

A combination of countries now in the British Commonwealth may claim to have given the world railways as it has also given it cricket.

As a matter of interest, Indian Railways is the biggest employer in the world: it employs 1.5 million people, comprises about fifty thousand miles of track and carries around one hundred million travellers a day. This is all a great development from the first little locomotive steam engine to pull passenger carriages, called *The Puffing Devil*, which Richard Trevithick (1771–1833) invented and ran up Camborne Hill on Christmas Eve 1801. This event inspired the Cornish folksong *'Camborne Hill'* when, three days later, the engine broke down and its driver and fireman retired for 'refreshments', leaving it to boil dry and explode – which is a better excuse for not running than 'leaves on the line' or 'the wrong kind of snow' (excuses used by recent British railway companies to excuse late running and cancellation of trains). The refrain of the song is:

> Going up Camborne Hill, coming down,
> Going up Camborne Hill, coming down,
> The horses stood still;
> The wheels went around;
> Going up Camborne Hill, coming down.

When this is sung in a Camborne-Cornish accent, importantly, the word 'going' is pronounced to rhyme with 'loin' and 'horses' is pronounced 'hosses'. The verses largely refer, with robust Georgian disparagement, to Lady de Dunstaville whose origins and habits were humbler than her title and who was unpopular because she was considered to be 'no better than she ought to be'. She was supposed to have been a witness to this first locomotive run. One of the verses is seldom printed – but always sung in Camborne – without saying too much, one of the lines in this verse is: *'It cost me a quid'*

142

The first fare-paying railway was established by Trevithick, in 1808, on a site, recorded by a plaque, at what is now Gower Street in London. The engine was called the *Catch-Me-Who-Can*. Richard Trevithick died (after many years spent in South America, from which he made little), completely unhonoured by his country and a virtual pauper. It is said, by some, that his gold watch paid for his funeral in Dartford, Kent, where his grave is still unmarked; others say that his work colleagues paid for the funeral. There is, however, a magnificent statue to him in Camborne; a monument to him in Merthyr Tydfil, in Wales, and the plaque in Gower Street.

European Sleeper Trains

The most famous of these has to be the Orient Express, which first made its journey from Paris to what was then called Constantinople in October 1883. The last regular train service was run in May 1977 but the carriages were later reunited and restored and it again runs special trips between various European cities: London, Paris, Dresden, Rome, Vienna, Venice, Budapest, Prague, Krakow and also Istanbul and, once a year, it still does the fabled full run, over six days and five nights, from Paris to Istanbul. Don't forget your moustache wax.

More prosaic but still exciting sleeper train services are still provided by a range of companies, between various European destinations. The main providers are: Lunea; Elipsos Trenhotel; Citynight Line; Lusitania; Artesia, and the Eurostar Direct Ski Train, which is a seasonal sleeper train, taking the British to the Alps.

Other Great Railway Journeys

One other great journey is between Islamabad and Lahore. The journey is three hundred kilometres and there are only two trains that run shuttle services in each direction but, believe me, whether you board amidst the turbulence at the great Victorian stations at Islamabad or Rawalpindi (the only stop) or at Lahore, there really is no better way to see these fascinating places and whenever I hear diatribes against British rule in India, I think that there should be more reflection upon the monumental engineering achievements which were left behind and still operate.

The Flying Scotsman still leaves King's Cross each morning at 10 am as it has for most of the period since the service was begun in 1862. The Edinburgh to London train leaves Edinburgh at 1 pm. *The Cornish Riviera Express* is still the late morning train, which leaves Paddington for Penzance, as it has since 1904. This service was made famous by the brilliant 1930s' advertising posters which helped to make it one of the world's most famous train services. 'GWR', really standing for 'Great Western Railway' was reinterpreted as 'God's Wonderful Railway'. The names and the traditions do make them special trains and lend a touch of romance to travel in this humdrum age.

Sea

The purpose of sea travel changed dramatically in the twentieth century: at its beginning, sea voyages were undertaken out of necessity to travel long distances and, by its end, the only journeys borne out of necessity were those involving ferries; for carrying cargo and heavy freight, or in connection with armed naval engagements and manoeuvres. This is not to say that sea journeys across the Atlantic and out to the furthest ends of far-flung empire did not evolve into journeys offering legendary luxury and fine things. But now the cruises on offer are designed to offer rest and relaxation and stop-overs in interesting locations; time is no longer of the essence and long gone are the duels between the great steamers of the 1930s such as the Cunard White Line's *Queen Mary* and the French Compagnie Générale Transatlantique's *Normandie*, competing for the blue ribbon (or riband), awarded for each year's fastest westbound transatlantic crossing to a commercial passenger vessel. Before this, from 1909 to 1929, the blue ribbon was held by Cunard's great *Mauretania*.

In their places, there are generally more localized cruises; although Cunard still offers transatlantic crossings of between six to eight days on the *Queen Mary 2*; the *Queen Elizabeth* and the *Queen Victoria*, as well as cruises to many destinations from Panama to Norway.

Some thoughts on suitable travel dress

Safari suit

A safari suit, in a traditional pattern is terrifically comfortable for wearing when travelling. The best cloth for this is undoubtedly Ventile, which is a proprietary name for a type of waterproof cotton, with an interesting history. In the Second World War, the British ran short of linen for making fire hoses and so an alternative cloth was developed from cotton. It was so successful that it was also used to make flying suits for the intrepid pilots of expendable fighter airplanes that used to escort the North Atlantic convoys until the 'planes ran out of fuel. These pilots then had to ditch their airplanes in the freezing ocean and take their chances of being picked up by the convoy before they froze to death. The

144

advent of Ventile flying suits undoubtedly saved many of their lives. You just match your safari suit up with a pair of comfortable, elastic-sided, slip-on shoes, which will expand as your feet swell. If you are going somewhere hot, take a sola topee or a panama hat; if somewhere cold, a heavy overcoat, a pair of peccary or deerskin gloves and a good felt or tweed hat.

Shalwar Kameez

For long-haul flights, I greatly favour (and recommend) the Indian Shalwar Kameez. This comprises a loose-fitting, cotton, tunic shirt (kameez), long to just past the knees, slit up part of both sides to the hip joint (which, incidentally, is the point at which to judge the best length for an umbrella, a stick or a cane). The kameez sits outside the shalwar, which is a pair of (enormous) 'all-size' or 'free-size', cotton bloomers, heavily gathered at the waist and fastened with a draw-string cotton belt; they taper to a reinforced seam at the ankle. Combined with a pair of embroidered Indian slippers (and no socks), you are dressed as comfortably as in a pair of pyjamas (which derive, in some measure, from this suit) but, with the addition of an armless gilet in worsted wool, equally ready to disembark and jump into a cab, anywhere in the world, without raising too many eyebrows.

Tropical evening dress

If you are off to a tropical place, where you are going to be required to wear evening dress, think about the possibilities that present themselves. First, you could just take along your regular dinner jacket (Tuxedo) in black or midnight blue. Secondly, you could take a white, ecru (off-white), stone-coloured or even dove grey, lightweight dinner jacket (either single or double-breasted), maybe with a shawl collar and lapels and wear this with the rest of black tie evening dress as described in *History of Men's Fashion*; but have a pair of lightweight dark evening trousers made. You might have this jacket in a gabardine tussore, shantung or dupioni silk, or mohair, with *self* collar and lapels (that is to say with no silk facings; although they are not incorrect, as such). Another option is to go for unbleached duck (linen). I should just add that this tropical evening dress is not usually worn outside the tropics, however hot it gets.

Where it becomes unbearably hot, the Royal Navy began (in 1800), the ultimate dressing-down for evening dress. This now is variously called *Red Sea Rig*, or *Gulf Rig* and comprises black tie evening dress without any coat or dinner jacket but with a cummerbund. There is no reason why a similar prescription should not be applied to civilian evening dress where the circumstances warrant it.

Shirtmaker Emma Willis recently mentioned the nice expression '*Gloucestershire Half Change*', to describe evening home wear comprising: a smoking jacket (or suit), velvet slippers and shirt without a bow tie (maybe with a cravat).

145

Polo coat

A very useful coat to have for sports' country wear and ocean or rail travel (even for polo, come to that), is a polo coat; supposedly devised for wearing between chukkas in the North West Frontier in the days of the British Raj; although sometimes it is called a 'tennis wrap'. Typically, this has now evolved to comprise a double-breasted style of top coat (either with a reversible style of collar and lapels, similar to an Ulster, or a standard double-breasted style) and with gauntlet cuffs, shoulder vents or a central vent in the back and a leather-covered buckle belt (often just loosely tied) or a half belt, flapped patch pockets, in natural camel hair cloth, quarter-stitched along all the seams and set off with large, white, shell (mother of pearl) buttons or buttons made from vegetable 'ivory' taken from the nuts of the Brazilian palm *Phytelephas macrocarpa*. A great example of this type of coat is worn by Leslie Howard, on an ocean voyage, near the beginning of David O. Selznick's 1939 film *Intermezzo*. However, it might be noted that some of the earliest players of the game of polo in the north-west frontier, by legend, used to use the severed heads of their defeated enemies as balls and were probably dressed in the shalwar kameez (already mentioned), together with a voluminous cashmere shawl, rather than any kind of coat, as such.

British Warm

This is a camel-coloured coat in a familiar pattern, deriving from a military design and, in its civilian form, includes leather-covered buttons and retains the military epaulettes and it is a versatile and useful item to have for travel.

More on hats

On the hat front, I ought to mention Bates the hatter, which has moved in with Hilditch & Key, out of the site from which it has traded for over a hundred years, to enable the Crown Estate, the freeholder, to undertake some destructive and wholly unnecessary re-development programme. Bates holds in stock the most varied designs of tweed trilby-style hats of the four remaining central London hatters.

Living Abroad

As the western economies flounder, many people think of getting away from it all for good. I certainly did. However, with the benefit of hindsight and with some dearly bought experience, there are things that I would have done differently.

First, I would not have made the seemingly small (but tremendously important) procedural error in the permanent visa application. The result of this was to make me a virtual prisoner in the country for several months (because, although the position was tolerated by the authorities, my residency became irregular) and, had I left, there was no guarantee that I could get back in to the place where I had made my home. Fortunately, this has now all been sorted out but at much avoidable expense of time, money, effort and patience (waiting in endless queues with other procedural defectives, to be dealt with by bureaucrats who seem to revel in finding as many additional points of difficulty as possible: all of which would test the patience of a saint).

You should fully understand the correct visa for which you should be applying (whether retirement or other type of permanent visa, such as an investment visa); the requirements of the process and where the visa will be issued (often you will have to leave your country of choice and return to your country of origin to collect it). If necessary, use a recommended visa expert to assist you but rely on *personal recommendations* and do not just pick a name from the directories held by the consulates.

Secondly, I would have been much more ruthless in discarding personal possessions in England and not left a containerful for shipment: this is costly to store and move and often cannot be imported into your new country until you have secured a right to permanent residency. I would have kept my clothes and some books and personal papers but the furniture would have all gone. Even when you get to the stage of seeing the container arrive, you may still face delay because there is doubt about whether an item may lawfully be brought into the country and then demurrage charges will start to build up in the port.

If you do decide to go, lock, stock and smoking barrel, make sure your electrical equipment really will not work in your new country, because this is what many a smart-alec will tell you. I was seriously misled about this and gave all my electrical goods away when, it turns out, there is a 240V electricity supply available here on request.

Do your arithmetic and make sure that, so far as you can tell, your income, from all sources, is going to be enough to keep you going, bearing in mind the recent inflation rates in the country of your choice.

Make sure that the new country does not have any tax on foreign investment. If it does, this can often be circumvented by establishing your own local company and using that as a vehicle for the purchase of any property or investments. However, often you will need a person with citizenship or residency to operate the company for you so make sure that you have someone trustworthy but, in any event, restrict their access to bank accounts and title deeds.

Foreign investment is one pass-key to obtaining residency in many countries but ensure that any investment that you are required to make remains your investment and is not appropriated by the government as a type of tax.

Try to find a country that is welcoming foreign investment and offering incentives to foreigners, such as tax breaks on income from local investments.

Go to your family doctor and ask about necessary vaccinations for the country of your choice and keep a record card for future reference.

Tell the Inland Revenue that you are becoming non-resident to avoid any future problems with them.

Notify your bank and any card-providers that you are going to be using their cards in the new country for the foreseeable future but also make sure that you leave open the possibility of using the cards in other places that you might travel to, or through.

Make sure that you invest in any new computers that you are going to need in Europe or North America and make sure that your mobile telephone will work; if it will not, buy one before you leave as this type of equipment is often costly in developing countries; the same thing goes for sunglasses and designer clothes.

If you are going to a country where a language that you do not speak is spoken, make sure that you at least learn enough before you go to deal with everyday matters such as shopping and dealing with the providers of necessary services. Moreover, the less you speak the local lingo, the more likely you are to be seen as fair game: a 'stupid gringo' or other local equivalent, in relation to commercial matters, and taken for a complete ride; before you work out that there is a discount for ready cash and that your new-found 'friend' who suddenly appeared and is helpfully introducing you to local tradesmen, is getting a ten per cent kick-back on sales to you and that this is being added to your bill. Before you buy anything or contract for the provision of local services, make sure that you establish the normal local market rates and if you are quoted more, make sure that you stick to your guns. Find out local customs such as discounts for ready cash, tipping for work done and follow the local customs; do not start recklessly splashing out or you will disturb the *status quo* and cause resentment.

Finally, unless you are entering a condominium full of ex-pats whingeing on about there being no fish 'n' chips (and I hope that you are not), remember that you are going to have to work hard at being accepted by the local community. Moving anywhere different brings an expectation that you might have to work to 'get in'. For example, I started going into a little bar down the road for cigarettes and, for several months, the owner appeared suspicious and behaved curtly, slamming the packet and the change down on the counter and moved on with other business. You just have to take it on the chin and wait for some opportunity to crack a little joke. The first glint of a tooth, behind the ghost of a smile, is the point at which you know that you are getting there and when, a while later, he waved to me as I passed, I knew that, in a sense, I had *arrived*.

CHAPTER 10

Some Unusual or Exciting Christmas Holidays

'God Bless us, every one!' Said Tiny Tim, the last of all.

The End of *A Christmas Carol*, by Charles Dickens

As with the rest of this book, this chapter is not, in any sense, meant to be exhaustive but, in the general spirit of the rest of it, just intended to stir enthusiasm and make a few suggestions.

Nova Friburgo in the Mountains of Rio de Janeiro and Something of Patagonia

This is a side of Brazil that the world seldom thinks about. But it is there all right (about one hundred and forty kilometers outside Rio de Janeiro, nearly three thousand feet up in the mountains called the Serra Fluminense).Here there are some mountain villages that could (but for the absence of snow), be in Switzerland. The area takes its name from Fribourg in Switzerland and the settlement of Swiss (and then later also German) people here dates from 1818. The original settlement was called Fazenda do Morro Queimado (Burnt Hill Farm). It was granted city status in 1890. There is a great place to stay called Parador Lumiar which includes thirteen separate chalets. There are opportunities for climbing and hiking and there is also an ecological park with several caves and a view of a rock formation called the *Sitting Dog*. In July, they hold a winter festival in the city and there is a culinary festival in September.

Obviously, it depends where you live in the world, because, if Switzerland is closer, you'll probably just go there. Certainly, if you are after snow you will need to go there rather than to this area, although, so far as that goes, there has been development of a skiing resort just outside São Paulo, with synthetically produced snow and ice. However, most Brazilians go skiing in real snow between July and August at Bariloche, Patagonia, Argentina. The El Casco Art Hotel is one of the best there.

Switzerland – St Moritz

Maybe this is the most exciting Christmas destination of them all. They say that Swiss winter sports for the international set began here in 1864 when Johannes Badrutt won a wager by persuading English tourists to come to stay and enjoy the winter sports and it has been home to the world famous and perilous Cresta Run for toboggans since 1885. The Kulm Hotel (dating from 1856) and Badrutt's Palace Hotel (dating from a remodeling and development by Caspar Badrutt of the Hotel Beau Rivage which had been built in 1872), provide the very best in accommodation, food and drink. The usual winter sports are available, as well as the polo on snow World Cup Championship, which takes place in January each year on the frozen lake. Badrutt's was possibly the last hotel on earth to require dinner jackets to be worn after 6pm; now this has declined to '*jacket required; tie desired*'. Surely, there was room for one *last* bastion of civilization, was there not?

Gstaad Valley

This is in Saanenland, which was once part of Gruyère, until the Count of Gruyère went bankrupt in the sixteenth century when it was ceded to the canton of Berne. The Gstaad-Saanenland Resort, including Pays d'Enhaut is situated on the French-German language border between Lake Geneva and the Lake of Thun. Besides the usual winter sports there are concerts, tennis events and there is Le Rosey educational institute. The Gstaad Palace Hotel is one of the great hotels of the world.

Lapland

Of course, this is where Santa Claus's HQ is based. When we were children I recall that we used to leave out mince pies, an orange and a glass of sherry for him by the fireplace and he always used to take this refreshment and just leave a few crumbs, a perfect spiral of peel and a dirty glass. I even once caught a glimpse of his coat disappearing around a corner, after he had made his delivery one year.

One hundred miles north of the Arctic Circle, in the town of Jukkasäjrvi, in Swedish Lapland is the ICE Hotel, built from blocks of ice produced by the river Torne. You will also find there an ICE church and ICE bar. Even the beds are made from ice (although lined with mattresses and reindeer skins and complete with thermal sleeping bags). There are no log fires or central heating here so take your silk long-johns and thickest furs. However, there are traditional, heated rooms available for the thinner-blooded.

If you really want the log cabin and fire experience, there is the Lapland Tourist Board to give advice.

Lebanon – Cedars

If you ever want to go to see the famous cedars of Lebanon, Le Cedrus Suites Hotel is a 40–room hotel situated in The Cedars Mountain and Ski Resort in North Lebanon, with every facility and tremendous views.

Lake Como

Villa D'Este is just north of Milan. It was originally built, in 1568, for Cardinal Tolomeo Gallio and is set in twenty five acres of magnificent gardens overhanging (rather than merely overlooking), Lake Como. For a while it was also home to George IV's exiled and scandal-ridden Queen Caroline. It has been an hotel since 1873 and, besides providing superb accommodation, even houses statuary from the school of Canova. Meals can be served just about anywhere.

Venezuela – Angel Falls – Canaima

The highest waterfalls in the world are certainly worth a visit. They are named after an American pilot, called Jimmy Angel, who discovered them in 1937. They fall from the Auyantepui into The Devil's Canyon, nine hundred and seventy-nine metres below, with an unbroken drop of eight hundred and seven meters. The most renowned hotel around here is Jungle Rudy Campamento, which has fourteen rooms and a thatched bar as well as spectacular views.

Murree

Murree in Pakistan, is about twenty miles north-east of Islamabad and stands at 7,517 feet above sea level. It was developed, at Sunnybank, from 1851, as a summer hill station and sanatorium in the Himalayan foothills by the British, partly to escape the heat of the central and southern lowlands and it enjoys a refreshing sub-tropical, highland climate. It also provided the summer seat for the government of the Punjab until 1876 (when that was moved to Simla). Its name probably derives from the Urdu for 'high place'. There is an area which, to this day, is laid out much in the design of a North London suburb, with 1930s' designed houses, surrounded by gardens and fragrant pine forests. The only things that give the game away are the spectacular mountain views (on a clear day, you can see more or less forever and make out the mountain Nanga Parbat, at 26,658 feet). Also noticeable are the clean air, the jacaranda trees, the wandering, distinctive kashmiri goats and the fact that the houses and the former British clubhouse are incongruously roofed (as is the church down the hill), with corrugated iron. Around Christmas time, there is often deep snow and a bit of a freeze and, when I was there, power cuts were a daily occurrence. There is now even a Hotel Pearl Continental, a five-star hotel, where a good welcome and a very reasonable degree of Christmas cheer can be found. A smaller but well-positioned and appointed hotel is the older (but renovated) Shangri-La Resort Hotel.

Murree is not a ski resort and if skiing is your objective and *provided that you are satisfied that it is safe again*, try Malam Jabba in Swat, where there is skiing to be had. The Foreign and Commonwealth Office advise on whether countries and areas are safe at any particular time.

This is Swat, as in Edward Lear's question:

Who, where, why and what is the Akond of Swat?

The answer appears to be that he was a local, ascetic, Sufi Muslim, tribal leader in the Swat Valley.

In Murree itself, watch out for the shops selling *khusse* (finely embroidered oriental slippers) and the fur and curio shops in the main bazaar on the Jinnah Road (also known as the Mall) as well as the little tailors' and seamstresses' shops, off around the narrow back roads, where they make, in a couple of days, bespoke shalwar kameez, hand-rolled silk handkerchiefs and tailored gilets for such small sums that you feel guilty to hand them over.

If you go on a trek into the Himalayan foothills that begin here, and are really lucky, you might even see the magnificent and secretive snow leopard (*uncia uncial*), which is, probably, on a par with riding on the backs of dolphins.

CHAPTER 11

Burlington Bertie – or Tramp for a Night

I'm Burlington Bertie, I rise at ten thirty,
And saunter along like a toff;
I walk down the Strand,
With my gloves on my hand;
Then I walk back again, with them off!

William Hargreaves

Ever been a tramp for a night? I have. It was at a time (AD 2000), when I lived in St James's Square. I don't mean that I lived *in* the square in the sense of living on a bench, midst the leafy London plane trees, hard by the statue of King Billy. I normally lived in a flat, high above the south side. Possibly, these are amongst the best sited flats in the whole wide world. But, one night, I did, perforce, actually sleep *in* the square.

It came about in this way: residents of the buildings in the square may apply to the trustees for a key to the gardens (which are locked to Joe Public between dawn and dusk, at the weekend and on high days and holidays). So I thought to myself: 'I'll have one of those' and I put it on my key-ring.

Occasionally, I vaingloriously wallowed in lounging around in there, after hours, to the consternation of Joe Public helplessly rattling the gates. Yes, it is true to say that I smirked at them. But one fine night (and, fortunately, it *was* a fine night), owing to some domestic dispute, with which every sporting man of the world is sadly familiar, I found myself out on my ear, with no cash, no cards, and my friends were all too far away to help, but I had my key-ring, with the Magic Key. So I thought, in my, admittedly, less than *lucid* state, that I would simply bed down, in my astrakhan-collared coat on a bench 'neath God's firmament, on a jolly old bench for what remained of the night. Safely in, I soon realized that this was a veritable colony of the dispossessed who, by divers means (loops in railings and conveniently over-hanging branches), managed to get themselves the first and best pitch in the little pavilion, on the south side. Unfazed by these trespassers (and sensibly unchallenging of their rights), I settled down and slept the sleep of The Just, on a bench on the west side.

I cannot say that it was an experience that I should care to repeat (after all, there is much to be said for marble-tiled bathrooms, running hot water, down-filled pillows and springy mattresses). But, in some curious way, it is not an experience that I would have missed for the world.

At dawn, some workmen renewed their noisesome efforts to renovate one of the adjoining blocks on the south side and quite spoiled an agreeable dream; so I thought: 'Demme! I need a shave – or I shall spend the day looking like Burlington Bertie!' Having been surreptitiously relieved of my street door key to the apartment block, a little ingenuity convinced me that I should borrow a screw-driver from the workmen (on some colourable pretext, which I forget). Mission accomplished (after all, who suspects a chap in an astrakhan-collared coat, in St James's Square, of burglarious intent at 6am, on a brisk morning?), and I easily (too easily) and Raffles-like, slipped the latch of the street door with a piece of plastic and went up in the lift to the top floor.

After padding along the corridor, I reached our door and carefully opened it with my key. As I had anticipated, the chain was still on but, deftly, I unscrewed the little blighter with my borrowed screw-driver and went in. I had a shower and a shave and made a cup of tea. I even left some in the pot for 'er indoors. Then I left, as I had entered, after having replaced the chain and, on my way off, I returned the screw-driver to the unconcerned workmen. This left me wondering: how many chaps who have legitimately lived in an abode in St James's Square have actually slept a full night through, 'neath that leafy canopy in its middle...?

I said that it was an experience that I would not like to have missed. This is because, lying there, on a bench, beneath the plane trees, by moonlight, various lyrics came to me; that had never hit me so much before, just lying on a springy bed, with down-filled pillows: *Maybe It's Because I'm a Londoner* (by Hubert Gregg, sung by Bud Flanagan); *London Pride* (written and sung by Noel Coward); *I Live In Trafalgar Square* (by C W Murphy and belted out by Stanley Holloway), and *I'm Burlington Bertie from Bow* (by William Hargreaves and charmingly sung by, amongst others, Ella Shields and Julie Andrews, parodying Harry B. Norris's earlier song *Burlington Bertie*, sung by Vesta Tilley).

The Spirit of London Town is a great thing and I surely encountered her that night.

Estado do Rio de Janeiro is a wonderful place to live (especially for tramps) but, needless to say, I kept that key.

Ask for the old paths, where is the good way, and walk therein, and ye shall find rest for your souls.

Jeremiah 6:16
Finis

Bibliography

Arundell, Dennis, *Story of Sadler's Wells 1633–1977* (David & Charles, 2nd ed. 1978).

Atkinson, John A, *British Duelling Pistols* (Museum Restoration Services, 1978).

Baldick, Robert, *A History of Duelling* (Chapman & Hall, 1965).

Barker, Harry, *Growing Fruit* (Mitchell Beazley, 3rd ed. 1999).

Barney, Sydney D, *Clothes And The Horse – A Guide To Correct Dress For All Riding Occasions* (Vinton & Co, 1953).

Baily's Hunting Directory (Pearson Publishing, annual publication).

Beerbohm, Max, *The Works of Max Beerbohm* (The Bodley Head, 1896).

Browning, Robert, *A History of Golf* (Reprint, A&C Black, 1990).

Buckingham, Louise, *Dunnages: Weavers, Hatters, Clerics, Colonists* (Louise Buckingham, 1937).

Burrard, Major, Sir Gerald Bart., *The Modern Shotgun* (Herbert Jenkins, 1944).

Burton, Sir Richard, *The Kama Sutra of Vatsyayana* (Translation with FF Arbuthnot) (Privately published, 1883).

Burton, Sir Richard, *Cheikh Nefzaoui's Perfumed Garden* (Translation) (Privately published, 1886).

Cullina, William, *Understanding Orchids: An Uncomplicated Guide To Growing The World's Most Exotic Plants* (Houghton, Mifflin, Harcourt, 2004).

Dallas, Donald, *Boss & Co* (Quiller Press, 2nd ed. 2005).

Daniel, Rev William B, *Rural Sports* (Longman, Hurst, Rees & Orme, 1812).

Flottum, Kim, *Complete and Easy Guide to Beekeeping: A Fascinating Reference With Recipes* (Apple Press, 2005).

Foulkes, Nick, *Last of the Dandies: The Scandalous Life and Escapades of Count d'Orsay* (Little Brown & Co, 2003).

Fox, Dr Nick, *Understanding The Bird of Prey* (Hancock House, 1995).

Fox, Dr Nick and Chick, Jim, *Falconry in The UK: An Audit of The Current Position* (Hawk Board Publications, 2007).

Freemantle, T F, *The Gun at Home and Abroad* (London & Counties Press 1912–1915).

Gladstone, Hugh S, *Record Bags and Shooting Records* (H F & G Witherby, 1922).

Gold, Richard M, *How and Why to Build a Wine Cellar* (Wine Spectator, 2nd ed. 1985).

Graham, Chris, *Choosing and Keeping Chickens* (Hamlyn, 2006).

Grahame, Kenneth, *The Wind in The Willows* (Methuen, 1908).

Hart, Robert A de J, *Forest Gardening* (Green Books, 2nd revised ed. 1996).

Hartley, J R, *Fly Fishing* (Hutchinson, 1995 edition).

Hogg, Dr Robert, *The Fruit Manual* (1st edition 1884; new edition: BiblioBazaar, 2009).

Johnson, Liz, *Orchids: Simple Steps To Success* (Royal Horticultural Society, 2010).

Kelly, Ian, *Beau Brummell* (Sceptre, 2005).

Kindersley, Dorling, *Vegetables in A Small Garden: Simple Steps To Success* (Royal Horticultural Society, 2007).

Loudon, J C, *An Encyclopaedia of Gardening* (Longman, 1824).

MacLean, Sir Fitzroy, *Eastern Approaches* (Jonathan Cape, 1949); *Tito* (McGraw Hill, 1980).

Marchington, John, *The History of Wildfowling* (Adam and Charles Black, 1980)

Ouseley, Sir William, *Travels in Various Countries of the East* (Rodwell & Martin, 1819).

Parlett, David, *Oxford Guide to Card Games* (Oxford University Press, 1990).

Phillips, Roger *Mushrooms* (Macmillan Reference, 2nd ed. 2006).

Pritchard, Col. DMC, *Pritchard's History of Croquet* (Cassell, 1981).

Quest-Ritson, Charles and Brigid, *RHS Encyclopaedia of Roses* (Dorling Kindersley, 2008).

Robinson, John R and Hunter H, *The Life of Robert Coates: Better Known as Romeo and Diamond Coates, The Celebrated Amateur of Fashion* (Samson, Low, Marston & Co, 1891).

Scarne, John, *New Complete Guide To Gambling* (Fireside, 1st printing of updated edition, 2005).

Shaw, Helen, *Fly-Tying* (Ronald Press Co, 1963).

Sitwell, Edith, *English Eccentrics* (Faber & Faber, 1933).

Sutherland, Douglas, *The English Gentleman* (Prion Humour Classics, new ed. 2001).

Thornton, J P, *The Sectional System of Gentleman's Garment Cutting, Comprising Coats, Vests, Breeches and Trousers* (Minister & Co, 1894, enlarged 2nd edn).

Walton, Izaak, *The Compleat Angler Or The Contemplative Man's Recreation* (Elliott Stock, Facsimile reprint of 1653 edition plus author's additions, 1897).

Williams, Michael, *Point-to-Pointing In Our Time* (Quiller Press, 1998).

Wilson, R L, *The Peacemakers: Arms and Adventure In The American West* (Book Sales Inc, 1992 reprint).

Newspapers and Periodicals

The Daily Mail for 29th July 1921
The Field (various).

Other Sources

Useful Internet Resources

www.basc.org.uk
www.country-alliance.org
www.cutterandtailor.com
www.englishcut.com
www.falconryforum.co.uk
www.falcons.co.uk
www.fieldandcountryantiques.co.uk
www.fishingbluemarlin.com
www.gofishing.co.uk
www.imfha.com
www.mfha.org.uk
www.mfha.org
www.panamas.biz
www.pointtopoint.co.uk
www.shooting4all.com
www.shootingUK.co.uk
www.silkroutescotland.com
www.sportingcollection.com
www.thelondonlounge.net
www.tweedjacket.com

Index

INDEX